FANTASTIC VOYAGE

A STORY OF SCHOOL TURNAROUND AND
ACHIEVEMENT BY OVERCOMING POVERTY
AND ADDRESSING RACE

LEE ROLAND

CONTENTS

IN PRAISE OF

This book charts one man's odyssey from humble beginnings to being a transformative presence in the lives of children and parents. It is a guidebook for those seeking to improve a damaged public school system that fails to address issues of race and poverty. It shows that change is possible. We need not acquiesce to a system that condemns our children to broken lives and limited futures.
—Dr. Nancy E. Snow, Professor of Philosophy, Director of the Institute for the Study of Human Flourishing at the University of Oklahoma

This book offers an honest assessment of the realities of life in our urban schools today, while offering practical insights to the character traits needed to be an effective leader in all settings. It will especially benefit those leaders who serve in school settings where children's futures hinge on strong servant leaders. *Fantastic Voyage* provides hope for those that have been entrusted to guide the lives of children that too many times are without hope. Lee Roland hit a home run with this practical guide for school leadership!

—Dr. Eric Jones, Superintendent, Jack-Madison County Schools, Tennessee

I have been a classroom teacher for thirty-five years. One of the major pet peeves that I (and all of my more-experienced colleagues) lament is the so-called "expert" advice we get year after year from people who have never been in the classroom on how to remedy the serious problems we face with regard to providing the best possible chance for our at-risk students to be successful. But when a man like Lee Roland comes along and walks into a school and orchestrates a turnaround such as the one at Tulakes, it ought to make everyone stand up and take notice. Because now we have moved from the theoretical to that which actually works. I think this book should be required reading for every educator and administrator. Instead of being theoretical, it's time we begin to look at what has actually been proven to work and start putting those principles into practice. To be blunt, this is a no-brainer.

—Jon Hazell, State of Oklahoma Teacher of the Year, 2017–2018

Teachers, parents, school administrators, and graduate students can sense Roland's tremendous sense of purpose. His powerful story of school improvement begins with his commitment to the calling of servant-leadership in his role as principal at Tulakes Elementary. As current and future educators read *Fantastic Voyage*, they will not only be thrilled with the story of an educational leader's success. They also will be given a template to use—with their own custom adjustments—to impact their classrooms and schools with positive change.

—Dr. Stephoni Case, Southern Nazarene University Educational Leadership Professor

Lee Roland is a retired educator, pastor, family man, community organizer, servant of God, and a trusted friend. He has devoted more than three decades of his life to serving at-risk youth and endeavoring to better the educational system in Oklahoma. His life and professional experiences involving failure, success, and the difficult struggle in between are beautifully illustrated in *Fantastic Voyage*. This book accurately portrays the reality of our inner-city educational system, as well as what we can do to positively change it. For those who have not experienced the struggles faced by poor at-risk communities, it is an eye-opening experience. For those who have, *Fantastic Voyage* is a sobering reminder of the truth.
—Major Paco Balderrama, Oklahoma City Police Department

Lee Roland is the "Man in the Arena." Through his ability to articulate who he is, where he came from, and how he pursued God's calling and purpose for his life, he gives the reader an invaluable guide to succeed as an educator. Teachers, principals, and administrators will be offered an honest, raw, and heartbreaking assessment of the human condition in many of the homes (and schools) of their students. Unlike many publications that just identify issues and leave the reader to deal with them, Lee Roland offers meaningful and well-vetted suggestions to address not only the symptoms of the issues, but also the root causes. My hope is that anyone who loves children and cares about the issues that effect them will read this book. Though Lee Roland wrote this book as a tool for educators, it should be read by everyone.
—David W. Prater, Oklahoma County District Attorney

Lee Roland is the kind of guy you wish had been your own kid's principal! *Fantastic Voyage* powerfully outlines a solution to the overwhelming challenges facing children in need. While so many of our community's kids are overwhelmed and underserved, hope can still shine forth from the school house. Failing schools would do well to listen to a man who took a failing school and made it soar. Thank you, Lee Roland!
—Wes Lane, founder of Salt and Light Leadership Training

There is a beautiful quote that states that true wisdom is born out in a life lived honorably, filled with good deeds done in humility. By that definition, Lee Roland is a truly wise man and *Fantastic Voyage* serves as proof. This book captures the story, experience, and soul of both his life and learning wrapped in practical love as a gift to the next generation of educators and administrators. I cannot recommend this book more highly and count it an absolute honor to join Lee in the continued fight to seek healing for an educational system that too often fails our most vulnerable.
—Caylee Dodson, Director, RestoreOKC

Lee Roland writes with a passion not for institutions or programs but for people, children, parents, and teachers. He writes with profound faith that his voyage can be ours if we have the will. It must be ours if we are to see our children—all children—flourish. *Fantastic Voyage* offers this invitation—come and see.
—Todd Wedel, Academic Dean and Rhetoric Principal, The Academy of Classical Christian Studies

This book is a must-read for any leader charged with the task of changing school culture and improving student achievement. Lee hits at the heart of what it takes to change a school culture for the

betterment of children. The stories and strategies Lee gives provide a framework to improve any school. Lee shares insight on how to make school a place children and teachers look forward to going to every day.
—Drew Eichelberger, Superintendent, Bethany Public Schools

As a police officer for the past twenty-one years, I can easily see the connections of crime, the prison population, and the failure of public education. In my view, Lee Roland is a first-line community crime fighter. This book is a refreshing blueprint to changing the landscape of our neighborhoods, schools, and communities. I'm thankful he gave us this model of self-sacrificing leadership to use in my area of influence!
—Lieutenant Wayland Cubit, Oklahoma City Police Department

Lee Roland doesn't just think about or talk about the crisis in education in our nation. He has demonstrated success in solving problems. If we, as cities, states, and a nation apply the principles of this book, we will see a transformation that will lead to our children and communities flourishing. Lee Roland's message is a lighthouse of hope so our ship can safely land. His example of bringing leadership and transformation to Tulakes Elementary provides a viable template that should be replicated across the nation.
—Scotia Moore, mother of ten children, Salt and Light Leadership Training Board Trustee

I am so glad Lee Roland has finally written a book to share his valuable perspective as an educator, community leader, and beloved mentor. From the day I met Lee, I could tell I would be blessed if I could maintain a friendship with him. I have learned

much from him and have been enriched by his life and friendship. If asked, I would gladly serve as the president of the Lee
Roland Fan Club. The world needs more Lee Rolands. I pray
this book is a path to developing more like him.
—Justin King, Oklahoma City attorney

This is an awakening. Some of the greatest pain and brokenness
comes from what we ignore and what we tolerate. For a white
woman who didn't even recognize the privilege that my biology
had given me, I heard my own voice of past ignorance echoing in
the pages. The opportunity of this book, read in soul-searching
sincerity, is that we can listen to understand, and speak to bring
unity. That indeed would be a worthy outcome.
—Susan Binkowski, Buy For Less executive

Fantastic Voyage is a book with heartfelt examples and principled
advice that cares about people. It challenges your mindset. Our
community can be better one child at a time.
—Greg Jones, entrepreneur and community advocate

Published by Gray Sparrow Books, an imprint of Storied Publishing.

Copyright ©2018 by Lee Roland

Permission requests and other questions may be directed to the Contact page at www.storied.pub.

Unless otherwise indicated, Scripture quotations are from the ESV Bible (The Holy Bible, English Standard Version), copyright 2001 by Crossway, a publishing ministry of Good News Publishers. 2011 Text Edition. All rights reserved.

Printed in the United States of America

Cover design by Sean Benesh

Interior design by Doug Serven

ISBN-13: 978-0-9973984-5-8

ABOUT GRAY SPARROW BOOKS

Sparrows are the humblest of birds. They represent the common person. We can't all soar like eagles or strut like peacocks.

Gray Sparrow Books seeks to give a voice to the humblest among us who have a message for the world. We think *everyone* should be able to hear from these thought leaders, storytellers, practitioners. We want to share their wisdom so we all can learn and grow.

Here's to these birds, these people, these ideas.

This book is dedicated to Wanda (Champ), Irv, and Chanel—my wonderful wife and absolutely the best son and daughter a father could ever ask for. Wanda, you have been amazingly helpful and supportive for thirty-eight years, from typing my papers with my small handwriting in college (on a typewriter!) to making me breakfast before I headed off to principal at 5:30 a.m., and more, so much more! Not only have you been an amazing support system, but you are three of the closest friends anyone could ask for. Thank you for allowing me the freedom to do the work I was put on this earth to do, to serve via public education and champion for America's most precious and vulnerable, our children, regardless of income or color. I love and appreciate you all so much!

ACKNOWLEDGMENTS

I would like to express HUGE appreciation to every Tulakes staff member that ever served with me, as well as the Tulakes community. Without you, there would have been no *Fantastic Voyage*!

Thanks to Pastor Robert Davis and LifeChurch NW Campus, David Ross and TriCorps Security, Pastor Mark Stapp and Cherokee Hills Baptist Church, CBRE, Sue Kuntze, Drew Eichelberger, John Lunn, and Chari Stratton for being there for me and Tulakes in so many ways. I am indebted and humbled by your patronage and friendship.

I want to thank the amazing Valerie Sherrer for contributing questions for this book and my editors, Julie and Doug Serven.

I owe so much to my late father, Dr. Dewitt Roland, my mom, Eula Roland, my brothers, Victor, Charles, Jerome, Vance, and Dewitt (especially for singing at special events, being a Watch D.O.G. and volunteer at Tulakes, bringing me an occasional burger, and being there for me whenever needed), and my precious little sister, Lornia, who has supported me from afar with prayers and always a listening ear.

I also have a big list of encouragers and friends who have meant the world to me over the years. Thank you: Kim and Brad Bandy, Pastor Clarence Hill, Wes Lane and my SALLT family, Lieutenant Wayland Cubit, Bea Jai Webb, Justin King, Dr. Stephoni Case, Dr. Lee Beaton, Pastor Jerry Lewis, John Rossi, the other members of the Fab Five from Star Spencer (Glen, Johnny, Dex, and Nate), Dr. Gloria Pollard and the class of '77 at Star Spencer, St. Luke Baptist Church, Kent Barber, Sargent Green, Kenny Deason, Rennie Cook, Linda Neal, Taylor Doe, Keith Jossell, Shannon and Tony Welch, Renika Veales, my colleagues in the Oklahoma City and Putnam City school districts, relatives, all of those who endorsed this book, and a host of others.

FOREWORD

CLARENCE HILL

More than twenty years ago, I met five children who changed my life forever. The oldest was thirteen and the youngest was about five. It took weeks for them to trust me enough to share their story. It was heartbreaking to learn the truth. Their father was a drunk, and their mother was on crack. They were basically raising themselves in an old two-story home in a state of serious poverty.

I remember how empty and powerless I felt. I knew enough about poverty and environment to gain a pretty clear mental picture of what their lives would become without some kind of direct and loving intervention. As a broke, twenty-one-year-old college student, I didn't know what to do. The food and clothes I came up with for them were only temporary. Who would make up for these missing parents, and who would help them have a better tomorrow? I wasn't much help at all, but their pain has caused me to spend my life looking for the answers that make the difference.

I finally found an answer.

His name is Lee Roland.

In twelve years at Tulakes Elementary School, Lee Roland created a path to a better tomorrow for children just like my little friends. How did he do it? The *Fantastic Voyage*. When I am around Lee, I am constantly taking mental notes about the amazing things he did to transform Tulakes from a school with the highest suspension rates in the district to a place of hope, where only one child was suspended in his last two years.

Lee helped me see that the goal of restoring strong families is essential for the long-term, but education done well is an immediate solution for kids. I believe Horace Mann is credited with the idea that "education... is the great equalizer." The classroom is one of our greatest opportunities to make a lifetime difference in the lives of our children. Lee has proved it is possible to create a healthy path for children in poverty. He reached students, and he impacted the lives of their parents. He created a school where the teachers don't want to leave, even though they had to make great sacrifices.

I met Lee Roland about ten years ago. This was during the time he served as principal of Tulakes Elementary with a "normal" twelve-hour schedule of 6:30 a.m. to 6:30 p.m. every weekday. He used his "free time" to speak to audiences about the experience of Blacks and children in poverty. I stumbled upon one of his events and didn't know what to expect.

In walked Lee Roland. Who was this black man with this military focus, and what was he going to say?

The rest is history.

I was blown away. His passion and his message were amazing. His presentation was so awesome that I've asked him to share the whole three-hour talk at our city conferences on justice. This man had answers.

I was determined to meet him. Our handshake was less than

a second, and he was out the door like a man on a mission. I said to myself, "If I ever get called upon to explain the plight of Blacks or of children in poverty, I'm going to point people to him."

Perhaps my thought was a prophecy, because the time came, and I kept my word. America again began to reel with the news of riots, marches, police shootings of unarmed black men, and even the KKK was back in the streets. Facebook was lit up with two very polarized opinions, and I found myself hosting gatherings, doing interviews, and being called into private meetings to discuss race with leaders in law enforcement, government, business, and media.

I didn't have to think twice about whom to call. I believe in showing up when it is time to speak, but I also believe in addressing problems with proven solutions. I knew a proven solution. His name was Lee Roland, and his proof was Tulakes—a thriving elementary school making a difference in the heart of concentrated poverty where almost 100 percent of the students received free and reduced lunches.

Lee, how did you do it?

How did you get white, middle-class female teachers to love their work so much that they enrolled their own children at Tulakes?

How did you succeed putting children who had been practically thrown out of other schools in the same classrooms with the regular student population?

This may sound unreal, but I've met the students myself. In 2016, the Oklahoma City-County Health Department co-hosted an international movement of leaders and change agents called 100 Million Healthier Lives. We made Tulakes Elementary one of the site visits. The group included superintendents, health professionals, and more. I will never forget sitting in the front office after the tour. They were blown away. Half of us were in tears because we could see our hope.

Hope is a reality. A bright future for our most under-privileged children is possible. This fantastic voyage can be anybody's voyage. This book will help you learn more about Lee. You will hear the stories and learn how to make a difference. You will be empowered to launch another fantastic voyage and make a difference.

INTRODUCTION

In general, public schools are making a failing grade, especially with children of color and low socioeconomic status. Despite all the new educational models, technological advances, research-based teacher evaluations, and reform efforts, our nation's public schools consistently fail this subgroup of children. Instead of one step forward, two steps back, I would argue our schools are instead moonwalking like Michael Jackson, gracefully gliding backwards.

As someone who has worked in public schools for the past thirty years, I believe this book will prove invaluable for educators, especially those who teach children of color and poverty. As you read about the turnaround achieved at Tulakes Elementary where I served as principal for twelve years, I hope with all my heart you will be motivated to confront and dismantle the brokenness that pervades our schools. We can—and must!—have a greater hope for tomorrow for ALL children.

It is my humble opinion that the vast majority of American

educators have all but given up on the idea of leaving no child behind. One writer notes:

> It's a familiar refrain in American education: African American children score lower on standardized tests, graduate high school at lower rates, and are considerably more likely to be suspended or expelled than the general population.[1]

I'll speak to how our public schools got to where they are and what is needed to lift them beyond their current, almost-universal despair. Educators nationwide have a thirst for answers to the problems plaguing inner-city schools. This book offers some solutions.

In addition to being a helpful and inspirational tool for educators at every level—from preschool to the university—*Fantastic Voyage* serves as a resource and guide for communities to know how to better love and serve their neighbors and advocate for sustained improvement in their local school systems. It also informs parents, the faith community, business leaders, policymakers, law enforcement—really anyone who is a stakeholder in education, which is everyone since the children are our future. My hope is that if we know better, we will do better.

The bottom line is *every* child deserves the best. Therefore, we *must* do better to provide quality public education for every child. I share about Tulakes not to boast about a bright spot but to encourage others to learn from and be inspired by our experience. If we did it, so can others!

Bookshelves are filled with topics on educational strategy, theory, and best practices for today's schools. *Fantastic Voyage* tells a simple story of how a public school overcame the odds and created a culture of success for all. It is not some pie-in-the-sky, theoretical, complicated approach for successfully educating children, but a factual and actual story, with examples that anyone could use as a blueprint. Anyone can follow step-by-step as I share how our school hurdled obstacles and implemented sustainable changes.

I was once a child in an at-risk public school system. I was Black, poor, and disadvantaged. Though I later went on to complete my master's degree, I personally understand the challenges of children from similar backgrounds. I also was once a bit of a "knucklehead," and thus I understand young knuckleheads. I also know that the poor knuckleheads have hopes and dreams too but may not have as many champions to cheer them on. So I became a champion for them and asked others to join me. I believe we created a foundation at Tulakes for many future champions.

Some of you reading this are victims of the current inadequate system. I want you to feel seen and empowered. Although you still have obstacles to overcome, I hope the Tulakes story will give you hope that positive change is possible and a vision for how that change might be created.

Educators and those in power *must* get a better understanding of and compassion for the powerless. *Fantastic Voyage* directly addresses the problem of race, poverty, and marginalization in our schools and society. The historic dance around these issues has been to the detriment of our country. We need to face the fact that we are and have been a nation divided. Only then can we make a conscious effort to unify. Only then can *every* child have a chance to succeed.

As I see it, a school can be likened to a ship on a voyage ferrying precious cargo from one destination to another. If the cargo were expensive wines, bullion, or anything else we deem valuable, it would be guarded and given every available resource to maximize a safe voyage. Heaven forbid it should capsize. If it did, no expense would be spared to retrieve the contents and document precautions to avoid a recurrence. However, when the ship's cargo is our children, especially the poor, it seems the concern is limited to only the parents of those children, who often at no fault of their own, are limited in their capacity to take the necessary steps to ensure the children's well-being.

Our children are much more important than wine, gold, or any of the manifold commodities we deem valuable. Any school in danger at sea requires and deserves our undivided attention and resources. Children's *lives* are at stake.

Let's start the voyage!

1
_____

LIFE BEFORE MY CAREER AT SEA

*None of us got where we are by solely pulling
ourselves up by our bootstraps. We got here because
somebody—a parent, a teacher, an Ivy League crony or a few nuns
—bent down and helped us pick up our boots.*
—Thurgood Marshall, first African American Supreme Court
Justice

My blessing and my curse is that I remember what it was like to be a kid. I can vividly recall the happiness, anticipation, and hope of almost every year from age three until now. However, I am also haunted by the fears, events, and adults who were larger than me and where I had no rights and no power. This was primarily in a place called school.

I want to share a journey that—if you'll take it with me— could end up infinitely benefitting children, especially those who are often outcast and marginalized. Autoethnography is a form of qualitative research where the author uses self-reflection and writing to explore personal experience and connect it to a wider cultural, political, and social context. Because I so deeply identify with children of color and low socioeconomic status (I grew up as one of them), I offer this autoethnography as a way for those with a different experience to approach such children with a more understanding lens. These also are the experiences that shaped me into the leader who took on the task of righting the sinking ship that was once Tulakes Elementary.

Family

I was born in Guthrie, Oklahoma, in 1959, the youngest of six boys with a sister two years younger than me. My dad, the late Dr. Dewitt Roland, was a Baptist preacher and pastor and incredible man. My mom, Eula Roland, is and has been an amazing woman and mother to me for fifty-eight years. These two people were extremely important players in my life.

There is an old rhyme: "Find a penny, pick it up. All day long, you'll have good luck." But in my childhood days, we weren't concerned about luck; we just never walked by any coin we saw on the ground. You see, I remember penny candy, and even two pieces of candy for a penny. I also remember not having even one penny to spend. My siblings and I would have gladly done almost any chore for any amount of pocket change, but being compensated or receiving an allowance for working around our house was not an option. We received room, board, hand-me-down clothes, and love. That was our pay, and we were generally content with the compensation. That's just the way it was.

I remember taking baths. We didn't have the capability to take showers. In fact, I did not know of anyone whose home was plumbed for a shower. We didn't take baths daily, but only when we were noticeably dirty or smelly (by Mama's appraisal, not our own). Baths were always taken on the eve of Sunday, and several of us used the same water. The plug wasn't pulled until you could no longer see the bottom of the tub. That's just the way it was.

I remember going to the drive-in movies. We almost never purchased snacks there. Mom made popcorn, which she put in a huge grocery bag, and we took a jug of Kool-Aid. We prayed for good weather so we could sit on the roof of the car for better viewing and hearing. If everyone had to watch from inside the car, it was nearly impossible to see since there might be nine or more heads in the vehicle. That's just the way it was.

I remember meal times, especially dinner, where we all sat down to eat together. There was generally enough, but seldom extra. If Mama cooked it, you were expected to eat it—everything on your plate. We heard, "You get what you get, and you don't throw a fit." We were constantly reminded that children in Africa were starving. Daddy would get his portion or selection first, and then we could be served. That's just the way it was.

I remember watching the one black-and-white television in our house. Our TV required adjusting the antenna countless times to watch one of the four channels available. Pliers were always nearby for the broken knob and aluminum foil to improve the antenna reception. The news came on each night at 10 p.m. with a message that said: "It's 10 p.m. Do you know where your children are?" Stations went off the air at midnight after a countdown and the playing of the national anthem. The programming educated and influenced me immeasurably regarding norms, values, and the American way. However, I absolutely cannot recall any shows that featured people of color. *Batman, Father Knows Best, My Three Sons, I Love Lucy, Leave it to Beaver*— none of them. That's just the way it was.

Family and church dominate my early memories. I grew up in and around extended family. One of my aunts and her two sons lived just two doors down. Other cousins, uncles, and aunts were frequently around as my father, even at a young age, was more or less the patriarch of the family, and our home was arguably the most stable. Our neighborhood was pretty nice for the times, filled with mostly Black, two-parent households, doing their best to achieve the American Dream. Overall, parents worked hard and kids played harder, outdoors from sunup to sundown.

We were always at church: almost all day on Sundays as well as revivals, choir rehearsals, Bible studies, workshops, suppers, trainings, and Vacation Bible School. Early Saturday evening, we began preparing for church. Saturdays started with a weekly ritual of hair cutting—to our parents' standards, not ours. We polished (spit and buffed and spit and buffed) our shoes until we could almost see our little black faces. We studied our Sunday School lessons as hard and as thoroughly as we would any subject matter for school. And on Saturdays we took our baths, whether we needed one or not. That's just the way it was.

On Sundays, we went to church in Spencer, Oklahoma, where my dad was the pastor. The church was little more than a one-room building, not much larger than a modest house. There was no indoor plumbing, so going to the restroom meant going to an outhouse, with a flashlight when it was dark—a daunting task for a child. Drinking water was brought in with a jug. When the water was gone, it was gone. We were warmed by a gas stove in the winter and by water coolers and paper fans on sticks in the summer. We were hardly ever warm enough or cool enough. And if our behavior was remotely inappropriate, we were sent to retrieve a switch (small tree branch) and received a good switching so we would learn to act more appropriately, or rather, not commit any act or mischief that would embarrass our parents (chewing gum, talking, sleeping, playing, etc.). I might add that as a preacher's kid, anyone could spank us, and many adults took that liberty. We were expected to be exemplars. That's just the way it was.

My father had grown up in a "po'" (that's *beyond* poor) family in rural Oklahoma, a son of a preacher and cook in the stockyards. He never graduated from high school. To help his family make ends meet, and with the outcome of World War II uncertain at best, he joined the US Navy at sixteen, lying about his age like many other young men in his day who wanted to help. After serving his country, he returned home, got married, and started a family. He and his first wife soon had four boys. Tragically, his wife died while giving birth to their fifth son. Later, my dad married my mom, Eula, and three more children were born, two boys and a girl.

My father was quite a man, role model, and champion to countless people throughout Oklahoma and the nation, but especially to me. He did not allow obstacles to discourage him. In fact, he apparently used difficulties as motivation and opportunities. He earned his GED, a bachelor's degree from Oklahoma Baptist University, a master's degree from Southwestern Theological Seminary, and a doctorate from Eastern Theological Seminary. He did all this while raising seven children and preaching and pastoring. He was so committed to learning and shepherding his flock that he was never satisfied with "good enough." Under his leadership, the churches he served flourished, far exceeding expectations. God used him, and he was all too willing to be used. He stood tall and was and still is my hero.

Mom was just a smidgen over five feet tall, and like my father, grew up po' in rural Oklahoma. And like my father, she too graduated from college at Langston University but for reasons you might not suspect. Mom was practically forced to go to college because her family didn't believe she could work fast enough in the cotton fields to hold her own. Her siblings thought blue-collar work of any kind would not be a fit for her. Thus, with meager financial support from home, she managed to put herself through college by cleaning houses for white families in the summer. Mom ultimately got her degree in what was then known as home economics. A few years later, she married my father and took up the reins of managing a large household.

I have unimaginable respect and admiration for my mother, on her own volition, becoming an instant mom to four young boys at the tender age of twenty-five, and against the urging of many family and friends. She ultimately raised seven children in the 1960s and '70s, and did so with incredible fortitude and faith. My mother, though small in stature, is a giant in character. She is unquestionably my "shero."

Together my parents made positive indelible marks on the lives of all my siblings and me. They maintained a model of marriage for each of us to strive for and emulate. Dad was the authority in our house. However, unlike some fathers, he said, "Do as I do, not just as I say." Mom was his capable partner. I only ever saw them demonstrate love and commitment to each other. They seemed in agreement on all matters of importance. There was no going to Mom and getting one answer and going to Dad and getting another. They never argued or fought in front of us. Their faith and devotion had an indelible impact on my siblings and me.

Confusing Times

We preach freedom around the world, and we mean it, and we cherish our freedom here at home, but are we to say to the world, and much more importantly, to each other that this is the land of the free except for the Negroes; that we have no second-class citizens except Negroes; that we have no class or caste system, no ghettos, no master race except with respect to Negroes? Now the time has come for this Nation to fulfill its promise. The events in Birmingham and elsewhere have so increased the cries for equality that no city or State or legislative body can prudently choose to ignore them.

— President John F. Kennedy, in a White House speech June 11, 1963

I remember walking home by myself from Edison Elementary School on November 22, 1963. I was four years old. Upon entering the den, I saw my mother and Aunt Julia crying while watching the old black and white television. Seeing the tears of these two endearing ladies was traumatizing to a little boy, but why they were crying caused me even more fear and confusion, then and in the days to come. The thirty-fifth president of the United States, John F. Kennedy, had just been assassinated in Dallas, Texas. As I recall, the people in my world, home, community, church, and school were all devastated. They saw hope for justice in the leader of this country disappear right before their eyes. However, that same black and white television showed footage of people in other parts of the country, particularly in the South, parading and celebrating in the streets. I was befuddled, to say the least.

In general, my young mind did not know how to make sense of the Civil Rights struggle. It was more frightening to me than *Frankenstein, Martians from Outer Space, The Creature from the Black Lagoon, Godzilla,* or anything else on television because it was real and happening to and around people I knew.

I remember Dr. Martin Luther King Jr. and especially the aftermath of his assassination. It was extremely scary. I remember

Bobby Kennedy and the aftermath of his assassination. It was bewildering. I remember Malcolm X and the aftermath of his assassination. It was horrific. I remember the riots of Watts, Detroit, Harlem, and more than one hundred other cities. It was terrifying. I remember the propagation of evil of the Black Panther Party, Huey Newton, and Bobby Seale. It was confusing. I remember the trumped charges and villainization of Angela Davis. It was perplexing. I remember the controversy and protest of America's participation in the Vietnam War, in which two of my brothers and cousins and neighbors fought. It was traumatizing.

I remember, on my ninth birthday, October 17, 1968, when Olympic gold medalist Tommie Smith and bronze medalist John Carlos were stripped of their Olympic medals in track because they lowered their heads and raised their fists, with black gloves on, during the medal ceremony. "Even if you won the medal," Carlos later said, "It ain't going to save your momma. It ain't going to save your sister or your children. It might give you fifteen minutes of fame, but what about the rest of your life?"[2] I was mystified.

I remember Cassius Marcellus Clay winning the 1960 Olympic gold medal, becoming World Boxing Heavyweight Champion, and changing his name to Muhammad Ali. I remember he refused to be inducted into the US Army for religious reasons and because of the mistreatment of Blacks in the US. Then he was stripped of his title. He only avoided imprisonment because he was financially able to battle the government in court. It was baffling.

I remember James Brown singing, "Say it loud. I'm Black, and I am proud," but not really feeling too proud or hopeful. I remember that to go to sleep at night, well into middle school, I would lay one arm over my face and rock my head from side to side. I remember, but I wish I could forget.

I also remember going on vacations as a family. We went to Detroit, New Jersey, Los Angeles, New Mexico, Kansas City, and Dallas. We did not "fly the friendly skies" of America and stay in five-star hotels and resorts. For vacations, we all nine loaded into our large Oldsmobile with no air conditioning and just AM radio. Most trips were nonstop, with Dad and Mom taking turns driving as needed. We always stayed with relatives upon arrival at our destinations. Mom would prepare as much food and drink as possible for the family to minimize spending and stopping, as there was a downside to both. For one, our funds were limited, especially for a family of our size. But also, Blacks were not welcome everywhere. Let's just say that not everyone was really civil during the Civil Rights struggle.

School

What I remember most about elementary school is saying the Pledge of Allegiance and singing "America the Beautiful" every morning. I remember recess, little boys dressed in rolled-up blue jeans, and little girls in dresses, black-and-white spats, and pony-tails. The teachers are somewhat of a blur, ranging from young, beautiful, urbane, and genteel to older, tough, and strong discipli-narians, but most all of them were Black. We were grouped according to our ability levels, particularly in reading. I wasn't in the high group (bluebirds), but not the low one (buzzards) either. As I recall, math was not a particular strength, as I did much of my adding and subtracting on my fingers for longer than I would like to admit. I remember that well up to third grade, school felt like a big maze to me everyday. I approached the opening of the school door each morning with a degree of apprehension, and I wondered if I would find the finishing line by the end of the day.

The teachers all had a designated teacher's pet whose primary job was to run errands and report any rule violations when the teacher was out of the room, especially if we had a substitute. This person, generally an attractive, light-skinned girl, wielded great power. I often despised this person and sometimes acted upon those feelings during recess, especially during dodge ball or kickball. I usually paid the price for it later when she would report that I was clowning or talking when the teacher was out of the room, even if I wasn't guilty. This would result in either writing "I will not talk" on the board a hundred times or worse—spanking with paddles or cut-off water hoses, taped on both ends. I got my share of whippings at school, which resulted in more of the same when I got home. I was a bit of a slow learner when it came to self-discipline and navigating school decorum, but I eventually got it.

Middle school was a different world altogether. We went from segregation to integration. We went from overgrown lawns and old, worn-out, broken materials to manicured lawns and new, well maintained materials. We went from going to a school where none of the kids had anything to going to a school where some kids seemed to have it all. We went from going to school with just the kids in our neighborhood to going to school with the kids on the other side of the street whose houses were strangely separated from ours with a road, a fence, and some thick evergreen trees. We had never seen or mixed with them, even accidentally, before then, nor had they with us.

I have little memory of the teachers, good or bad, in those middle school years, but I do know they were almost all White and had little to do with the children of color. One exception was our music teacher, Mrs. Sylvia Driggins, a beautiful, classy, young, black lady. For reasons I never knew, she was fired in the middle of the semester. I was so upset that I was disruptive enough with her replacement to get kicked out of class. Overall, though, I was a B+ student and navigated the academic world pretty well. I had white friends and foes for the first time in my life. Some of us snarled and fought on occasion, while others of us played and worked together without incident.

As one would expect, high school was another world. It was the late 1970s. Due to forced busing and integration, my high school in Oklahoma City (like many others) began to experience "white flight." Caucasian families moved to the suburbs in droves. The kids were integrating pretty well, but some of us were bringing our family values, beliefs, and issues to school. When those issues clashed, it resulted in catastrophic turbulence. The mostly white staff generally took one side, but in their defense, they were between a rock and a hard place. The black teachers were largely silent, but in their own catch-22. White parents took their children and dissipated like clouds. One of my saddest discoveries was finding that friends who I had from sixth through twelfth grades were there one day but gone the next, never to be seen or heard from again. We lost touch forever because of societal problems and beliefs that we had nothing to do with.

Another hurtful memory is that although I maintained a 3.5 grade point average throughout high school, I received little guidance or support from my school counselor regarding what to pursue beyond high school. In her words, the counselor said, "Lee, you should learn to do something with your hands, like woodworking or the like." I was flabbergasted. I'm not above such work, but I have never in my life been known for my handyman skills. When I told my father of the counselor's career advice, he was vexed, as he knew I was capable of doing things with my mind. He intended to accost that counselor, but it never happened, which was fine with me because I did not anticipate it going well.

So I was getting ready to graduate high school at the ripe age of seventeen. I recall January through May of my senior year as the most terrifying time of my life because I was clueless of the prospects for my future. Poverty has that effect. I remember telling my friends that I was going to attend the College of William and Mary after graduation. I did not have a clue where the school was, but it sure sounded prestigious, even though I knew my parents couldn't afford to fund my education there or really anywhere. I knew the military was an option, but I abhorred the idea of someone of the dominant culture yelling and cursing directives to do push-ups, pull-ups, or run just because he could. Alex Haley's *Roots* miniseries came out that year, further exacerbating my black, skinny, teenage angst. In what should have been a time of discovery, adventure, and carefree fun, I drifted day to day in my own *Twilight Zone,* wondering what the next chapter held.

College

I did not make it to William and Mary, but after selling my little 1976 Pinto and my mom writing grant proposals on my behalf, I was accepted to a state college, which I was just as proud and happy to attend. My four years at college then became both my best and worst years academically and socially.

Let's talk about the good first. In the fall of 1977, I enrolled at Oklahoma State University in Stillwater, Oklahoma. My oldest brother had gone there after his discharge from the US Air Force and earned a degree in electronic technology. I was hoping to follow in his footsteps and take the world by storm, or at least live a different life than the one I grew up living. I lived in the dorms, rooming with my best friend since elementary school. I was away from home and had the prerogative of doing almost anything I wanted. I could attend NCAA Division I football and basketball games that I had previously only been able to view on television. I could join a fraternity and be part of the esteemed and elite on campus. I could join movements or causes I believed in. I could date and have a girlfriend that lived on campus. I was in a place of higher learning. I was on a college campus and filled with ebullience and hopeful expectation.

Now for the not-so-good. I thought I was ready for adulthood, but quickly discovered I was just a youth and clueless about the world of academia, campus life, and society at large away from the security of my family and the people of my community. I also lived with the disquieting thought at the back of my mind that continuing to fund my education would be a tall order. It was one thing to get to college but another thing to stay there and graduate.

Nonetheless, my first week on campus, I attended a black student orientation where a black, confident, female older student attempted to enlighten the incoming freshmen on how to navigate and succeed in a place where many Blacks could easily find themselves failing and feeling like foreigners. As I recall, she said that Blacks numbered only 500 or so of the 23,000 students on campus, and that some of the 500 were commuters from nearby towns or international students from Africa. Therefore, having someone in class and in the dorms who shared similar backgrounds and culture would be few and far between.

In class I soon discovered my naiveté and that I was not as prepared as I had thought. I was not accustomed to being one of two or three, if not the only black student in class. I had never experienced loneliness, especially with people all around me. I had never had to work hard to make good grades and succeed. Therefore, after doing poorly on a few early exams and realizing that I apparently had not been appropriately prepared for college, I had a paradigm shift. I knew I was going to have to work my tail off to achieve my goals. Not one of my professors or anyone else in positions of influence or leadership looked like or appeared to identify with me in any way. However, the greatest shock was that the instructors, professors, and academic advisors did not seem to care at all whether I succeeded or failed. I was just a number and not a name.

For instance, my advisor enrolled me in an advanced electronics class, which I never should have been in as a freshmen with no prior technical experience. My classmates were all two to three years older than I, many with some military technical experience. To make matters worse, one day I dozed off in class after staying up too late the night before playing spades with friends. I was awakened by the thump of an eraser hitting me square in the face and classmates laughing their heads off. As the only black student and with chalk on my face, I felt both mortified and acutely alone.

Just walking to and from class was stressful. I remember so many times not seeing one person of color traversing either way. Big cowboys, with hats and boots, would walk four abreast on the sidewalk. They would never move to the right to allow me to get by. Therefore, the only option was to start a confrontation or to walk around them on the grass. Before the end of that school year, I promised myself I was not going to move off the sidewalk as it belonged to everybody. It was a promise I broke daily after realizing it was not worth starting fights all day everyday, especially with such odds against me.

On another occasion, I was sitting in algebra class, but I didn't have a pencil. I asked a white male sitting next to me if he had a pencil I could borrow. He promptly said, "No, I don't have an extra pen or pencil." He then opened his notebook to show at least a dozen pencils and even more pens. He retrieved one for himself, closed the notebook, and all but winked at me.

Most important and poignant of all, I remember the overall sense of never feeling like I mattered, or worse, even existed, to the faculty and staff at the university. I never missed class and almost always sat on the front row. Yet, the attention I received during class was minuscule at best. I do not recall ever being greeted in class. I do not recall getting eye contact in class. I do not recall being prompted and probed during class.

After having tests and papers returned, I was unpleasantly surprised by the grades and scoring on my research, essays, and exams. Then I would be shocked after glimpsing the higher scores and grades of classmates who seldom attended class and finished three-hour exams in as little as fifteen minutes. To put it mildly, I was dismayed and discouraged. I felt like I was an immigrant in my own country.

The whole environment seemed void of anyone who could identify with any portion of my existence. Very few noticed me or others like me. I felt like a bother or, worse, invisible. I was a kid less than one hundred miles from home, but that felt like I was a million miles away. I put on the confident and cool face of a young extroverted "brotha," but inside I was scared and lonely. I had numerous other such experiences during that lone freshman year in an era some might call the good old days. Those days did not feel so good to me, and to many others who looked like me.

I decided before my sophomore year to transfer to what was then Oscar Rose Junior College in Midwest City, Oklahoma (now it is called Rose State College). This resulted in the best educational experience I had after high school as far as feeling welcomed. There was a real sense of community. Plus, I lived at home with less financial stress and was able to work my way through school as I also worked a full-time job.

I married the girl of my dreams, Wanda, during this time as well, and we soon had two beautiful children. After completing junior college, I enrolled at what was then known as Central State University in Edmond, Oklahoma (now it is called the University of Central Oklahoma). I worked during the day and took courses in the evenings. My workload and family caused some detours, but I would not do anything differently. In fact, I do not know how I would have ever survived college if it had not been for Wanda's love, encouragement, and support.

A couple of moments stand out from that time in college. I took a math exam and missed only two of the thirty questions, which should have been an A. Instead, the professor marked "Cheated" on my paper and gave me an F, as a couple of my classmates apparently missed the same questions. He told me I must have cheated. My consternation was beyond belief, as I did not even sit near the other students. I protested to him as well as the dean, but to no avail. I had to retake the test, in which case the best grade I could make was a C.

Another incident involved my student teaching assignment. As teachers in training, we were directed to submit our top three choices of schools. My three choices were all within relative proximity of my home. The respective schools and administrators I'd chosen had preapproved me. Yet, I was not granted any of my three choices and instead was assigned a school I hadn't selected and far on the other side of town.

When I asked my classmates about their school assignments, none were denied all three of their top choices. I contacted the dean and asked if my placement could be reconsidered, especially since I was working an average of fifty hours per week and married with two small children. I was told, "Lee, if this is a conflict for you, perhaps you should wait to complete your student teaching, because you obviously have your priorities in the wrong place at this time." I retorted with a rationale to the contrary as I had worked hard to achieve my goal, but my plea fell on deaf ears.

While not all of these experiences were what I would have chosen at the time, they all served to shape the person and leader I have become, sympathetic and a champion for ALL. They also profoundly shaped the way I view and interact with the children and families in my care.

If a country is to be corruption free and become a nation of beautiful minds, I strongly feel there are three key societal members who can make a difference.
They are the father, the mother, and the teacher.
—A. P. J. Abdul Kalam, 11th President of India

DISCUSSION QUESTIONS FOR CHAPTER ONE

1. What exposure have you had to the stories and realities of those who lived through times of segregation and forced integration? How do you see the thinking of the pre- and post-Civil Rights Movement affecting us today?

2. What value would you place on the guidance a student receives throughout his or her educational experience?

3. Whose responsibility is it to address socioeconomic and racial inequities?

4. Do you care about your students' futures? If so (and I imagine you do or you wouldn't be reading this book!), how can you show them you care and not be perceived as indifferent or complacent?

5. What memories the author shared are similar to your own experiences? What memories are different from your experiences?

6. Do you remember any significant or painful life

events that you see now shaped your perspective and choices? How do you see them affecting you now and in the past?

7. What words would you use to describe your "beginnings"?

2

BECOMING A SKIPPER

A man who wants to lead the orchestra
must turn his back on the crowd.
—Max Lucado, author and speaker

My career as a professional educator began in the Oklahoma City Public School District, the same district where I attended school from kindergarten through commencement. At the time, it was the second largest school district in our state and one that had changed substantially just during the time I was in college. It was once a proud and heralded school system academically, athletically, and otherwise. It was the training ground for many celebrated state and national leaders, many of whom are noted as OKCPS Wall of Fame Humanitarian Award Honorees. The lists of doctors, lawyers, judges, politicians, athletes, business people, civil rights leaders, artists, educators, entertainers, and others is jaw-dropping, especially for a small Midwest city like ours. And there are many more who have not yet been recognized for their significant contributions. The list below gives just a sampling of the leaders OKCPS once produced.

- Bob Barry, Sr.—Legendary radio and television sportscaster and father of Bob Barry Jr., a legend himself
- Skip Bayless—Sports columnist, author, and television personality
- B. C. Clark Jr.—Successful entrepreneur and jeweler
- Ralph W. Ellison—Best known for his novel *The Invisible Man,* which won the National Book Award in 1953
- Prentice Gautt—First black football player and running back for the University of Oklahoma football team who went on to play in the NFL
- Vince Gill—Country singer and songwriter
- Joyce Henderson—Civil rights leader with Clara Luper as her mentor. She also taught and was a principal with Oklahoma City Public Schools.
- J. Clifford Hudson—Chairman of the board and CEO of Oklahoma City-based Sonic Corp.
- Kirk Humphreys—Mayor of Oklahoma City
- Wanda Jackson—Singer, songwriter in the mid 1950s and 1960s and one of the first popular females in the industry, known as the "Queen of Rockabilly" and "First Lady of Rockabilly"
- Willa Johnson—Oklahoma City Council member for fourteen years before becoming a County Commissioner
- Eleanor Blake Kirkpatrick—Founder and trustee of the Kirkpatrick Foundation and recognized as

Woman of the Year in 1962 by the Oklahoma
Chapters of Women's Radio and Television

- The Honorable Vicki Miles-LaGrange—First
  African American woman to be sworn in as US
  Attorney for the Western District of Oklahoma and
  first African American woman elected to the State
  Senate
- Bobby R. Murcer—Major league baseball outfielder
  who played seventeen seasons between 1965–1983
- Allie P. Reynolds—Major league baseball pitcher for
  the Cleveland Indians and New York Yankees
- Horace Stevenson—Owner of eight McDonald's
  franchises in the Oklahoma City and Tulsa areas
- Stanton L. Young—President of Young Companies,
  which included Pepsi-Cola franchises, and various oil
  and gas companies, commercial, and real estate
  ventures

This school district has produced some amazing men and
women! Yet like many urban school districts in the country, after
a well intended effort to reduce segregation in Oklahoma City
(forced busing in this case), the district was a victim of white
flight. The result was fewer children in our public, urban schools,
which meant not only a reduction of children but also a depletion
of resources.

Oklahoma City's newspaper *The Oklahoman,* had this to say
in a 2011 article:

In 1971, the district was near its peak enrollment with 71,000
students. The next school year a court-ordered busing plan
took thousands of students out of their neighborhood schools
and sent them across town. Within 10 years almost 30,000

white students left the district. About 2,000 black students left too.[3]

Since those former glory days, the district also has been the victim of "black flight." Many Blacks have since vanished from the boundaries of the district for the 'burbs and greener pastures. They too have added to the desolation of resources, talent, and people in the urban district.

Sadly, the Oklahoma City Public School District may never recapture its glorious past. At the very least, without laser-like intentionality, accompanied by tremendous support and resources, future stars may be few and far between. The district has certainly changed, enduring far less fame and fortune. However, I refuse to give up hope!

Latinos now make up the majority ethnic group (about 55 percent of the total population), followed by African Americans, and then Caucasians. A district that was once primarily White with a good mixture of economic ranges is now racially diverse with predominantly low socioeconomic families.

By the time I graduated from college in 1977, my once-almost-all-white high school was approximately 40 percent African American. By the time I started teaching, there were dramatically fewer Caucasian children, and the socioeconomic conditions were plummeting.

Training Ground

I began my career as a special education teacher in one of the three elementary schools in my hometown, the tucked away city limits of Spencer. When I was a kid, it was segregated and had all-white teachers and all-white students. But since then it had been desegregated and was nearly all Black. I marveled at the fact that I could not have attended school there as a child, but now I was a teacher there and that all-white population was almost gone. Wow, how times had changed!

In my field of certification, called Seriously Emotionally Disturbed at the time, there was never a dull day, which was perfect for a passionate and high-energy person like me. My students had so many challenges. They varied by race, age, gender, and socioeconomic status. But they almost all were either from single-parent homes, not living with either biological parent, or in the care of the Oklahoma Department of Human Services. Most, if not all of them, had suffered abuse or neglect of some kind. Without exception, they all had experienced significant trauma. They had seen, heard, felt, and experienced things that no human should endure, much less a child.

One boy's father had been married six times, and his last wife (#7) left on the boy's seventh birthday. It devastated him, and his behavior showed it. Another child had been alone with a parent who committed suicide. It devastated him, and his behavior showed it. Another child had suffered the most unimaginable sexual abuse. It devastated him, and his behavior showed it. All of those kids had experienced unthinkable emotional or physical distress in some form, and their behaviors showed it.

The histories of my students' behaviors prior to entering my program are not for the faint of heart. Spitting, hitting, biting, stealing, running, profanity, defiance, and intentionally urinating and defecating were par for the course. I spent the first day with one of my new students on the roof of the school threatening to jump, long before I ever saw the movie *Lean on Me*. I told him I would jump first and provided him with a graphically detailed description of my probable injuries when I hit the ground. He eventually talked me out of it, and we both climbed down safely. On another occasion, one of my students jumped out of a van traveling fifty miles per hour. Due to his injuries, he never returned to school.

Overall, my students had driven their previous teachers to delirium, even causing some to leave the profession, and not necessarily at the end of their contract year; they just quit on the spot. They were in grades kindergarten through sixth, and their needs and issues varied even more. My learning curve was so steep those fours years. The biggest thing I learned was that every child is unique and needs adults and educators to understand and care, regardless of his or her home life and regardless of physical appearance, behavior, or performance. The onus was not on them, the little people, but on the adults, the big people.

Those days are archived in my memory with pride and joy as our special education program enjoyed a great deal of success and was known throughout our district for caring for children well. Many kids who had known nothing but failure and chaos came to our program and learned to better self-govern their behavior while also achieving academically. I took great pride and joy in the fact that almost every single one of them left our program appreciably better than he or she had come.

I enjoyed teaching, and I envisioned continuing to do so, along with coaching, until my career was over. I had no aspirations of being a principal. In my mind, being a school administrator was on par with the lofty ambition of being elected governor (which really would be a huge deal in Oklahoma). I was raised to respect all adults, but I absolutely revered educators. Who was I to think I could lead and supervise teachers, one of the most important professions in the world? I had my internal ranking of God first, parents second, teachers third, and then everybody else.

However, teaching was not my long-term destiny. My administrators saw something in me and encouraged me to become a principal. They wanted me to start a new voyage. So I went for it. I completed my master's degree from the University of Oklahoma. I honed my skills of instruction and classroom management. I mediated parents and teachers while participating in Individual Education Plans as part of a team.

I was subsequently launched into the wonderful, wacky world of administration. I was ready to be a pugilist for the education and well-being of all children, including those most in need. I vacated the known for the unknown. I transitioned from security to insecurity. I traded a place where I would influence the lives of hundreds of children to impacting the lives of thousands of children.

Becoming an Administrator

My first administrative role was at a fifth and sixth grade center in the district. I was baptized by fire in this position. I saw teaching at its best and worst. I encountered teachers who loved and mastered their crafts and others who were apparently there for all the wrong reasons. I interacted with students and parents who ran the gamut as well. Some had it all together, while others were in a constant state of oblivion. I was cutting my teeth.

After a year as an assistant principal under my mentor Dr. Lee Beaton, I was assigned as head principal at an elementary school with an incredibly divided staff. The teachers were in an "us versus them" relationship, primarily younger versus older. The issues were unprofessionalism, territorialism, trust, and outright disdain for one another. The toxic situation required an equal employment officer spending an unprecedented entire week investigating allegations of employee impropriety at the school prior to my arrival. The departing principal was so unnerved that she voluntarily took a demotion in another school district. As she described both her futility and frustration, I didn't know whether to feel more sorry for her or myself.

Thankfully, my instinct and upbringing served me well. Those days of watching my dad pastor the church were invaluable. All I knew to do was what was right and what was in the best interest of the children. I lovingly preached professionalism to the staff and inspected what I expected. Anyone not with the program grew tired of hearing unity and oneness, but I never wearied in insisting upon it. Some of the staff who insisted upon working against the proverbial grain were cajoled, encouraged, and prodded with kindness and fairness. Some came around; others didn't. Those who did not acquiesce to my vision did not stay long. They went elsewhere, and I wished them well.

It was at this time that I first learned of the work of Dr. Roland Barth. Barth has a stellar resume as a principal, faculty member of the Harvard Graduate School of Education, founder of The Principal's Center, consultant, and author. I wholeheartedly embraced his assertions and incorporated his ideas with intentionality. He writes:

> The nature of relationships among the adults within a school has a greater influence on the character and quality of that school and on student accomplishment than anything else.
>
> If the relationships between administrators and teachers are trusting, generous, helpful, and cooperative, then the relationships between teachers and students, between students and students, and between teachers and parents are likely to be trusting, generous, helpful, and cooperative. If, on the other hand, relationships between administrators and teachers are fearful, competitive, suspicious, and corrosive, then *these* qualities will disseminate throughout the school community.
>
> In short, the relationships among the educators in a school

define all relationships within that school's culture. Teachers and administrators demonstrate all too well a capacity to either enrich or diminish one another's lives and thereby enrich or diminish their schools.

Schools are full of what I call *nondiscussables*—important matters that, as a profession, we seldom openly discuss. These include the leadership of the principal, issues of race, the underperforming teacher, our personal visions for a good school, and, of course, the nature of the relationships among the adults within the school. Actually, we *do* talk about the nondiscussables—but only in the parking lot, during the carpool, and at the dinner table. That's the definition of a nondiscussable: an issue of sufficient import that it commands our attention but is so incendiary that we cannot discuss it in polite society—at a faculty or PTA meeting, for example. (For more on this topic, see my article "The Culture Builder" in the May 2002 issue of *Educational Leadership*.)

Consequently, the issues surrounding adult relationships in school, like other nondiscussables, litter the school house floor, lurking like land mines, with trip wires emanating from each. We cannot take a step without fear of losing a limb. Thus paralyzed, we can be certain that next September, adult relationships in the school will remain unchanged. School improvement is impossible when we give nondiscussables such extraordinary power over us.[4]

With Dr. Barth as my guide, I eventually was able to usher the staff to a more respectable level of harmony and professionalism with approximately 90 percent of them ostensibly working happily together. Discord was minimal, almost negligible. In the end, the staff was much more of a team. We established a great climate and culture, and the students were achieving at a higher level.

Area Superintendent

My success at the school led to a promotion to central office as one of ten area superintendents. We worked in teams of two and reported directly to the superintendent. We were tasked with supervision of the hundred-plus schools in our district, elementary through high school, with a fairly equal assignment distribution among the five teams.

I was initially excited about this role because our job descriptions called for us to be in schools four days out of the week, overseeing and sharing our secrets to success, assisting principals to be more effective leaders in their respective schools. I was going to be able to help my colleagues. I was going to be able to help teachers. Most of all, I was going to be able to help more students. Or so I thought.

The two years in this role were the worst of my educational career when they should have been two of the best given my status and remuneration. However, we went from being in schools from four days to three, from three days to two, from two days to whenever we could. The job became much more of a chore, doing things I did not believe in and which I did not enjoy. Moreover, I saw leaders cut corners. I saw leaders serve themselves. I saw politics in its worst form, with children being used as pawns and ultimately the recipients of chaos and failure.

After two years, the state suffered one of its biggest budget cuts ever. Our district was hit exceptionally hard, and a new superintendent was hired. We already had been reduced from ten area school liaisons to five. The five remaining were all asked whether we wanted to return to schools as building principals or take our chances with possible reassignments to various departments.

Two of the five raised our hands, and I was one of them.

Being others-focused instead of self-focused changes your worldview. Living in a selfless manner and seeking to help others enriches our very existence on a daily basis. Get your hands dirty once in awhile by serving in a capacity that is lower than your position or station in life. This keeps you tethered to the real world and grounded to reality, which should make it harder to be prideful and forget where you came from.

—Miles Anthony Smith, author and speaker

DISCUSSION QUESTIONS FOR CHAPTER TWO

1. What impact do you see the home or family situation having on a special needs child or any child? What can we do about this?

2. What feelings have you experienced when transitioning from the known to the unknown?

3. Has there ever been a time when your capacity for leadership and impact caused you to transition to a new role or career? How did you feel? What did you realize through this experience?

4. What can leaders do to increase the probability of success for their organizations?

5. Who is at fault with the downward spiral of many of our urban schools, and what if anything can be done?

6. Have you ever considered the idea of a matter being "nondiscussable"? What examples of this have you seen? What can be done about the nondiscussable matters affecting our children's education?

3

THE SHIP'S CONDITION

Poverty is the parent of revolution and crime.
—Aristotle, philosopher

I became principal at Tulakes Elementary School in Northwest Oklahoma City (in the Putnam City School District) a year after my time as an area superintendent. I was immediately stupefied.

I had no idea this district that adjoined Oklahoma City Public Schools had any significant representation of people of poverty or color. I hadn't known there was a need for someone of my passion, fervor, drive, or color. My surprise was largely due to the district's perceived reputation. The Putnam City School District was known for its rich heritage and predominantly Caucasian, middle-class population. It was one of the districts on the receiving end of white flight.

First Impressions

To my surprise, there was indeed a need for my *Lean on Me*, Joe Clark-like spirit. The area surrounding the school was laced with Section 8, low-income apartments, many of which could and perhaps should have been condemned. Apartment fires and other safety issues were constant. In fact, if the disrepair that could be seen from the outside of many of the units was any indication of the conditions inside, some probably shouldn't have been lived in at all.

I had never laid eyes on that many apartments in one area in Oklahoma. I had seen similar living communities in high-population cities like Los Angeles, Chicago, and New York City, but I didn't know such conditions existed in Oklahoma City. My feelings from that first drive through the neighborhood would stay with me the next twelve years as I sought to be a fierce champion for those kids and families as principal at Tulakes Elementary.

The school's image and recent failure was on par with the neighborhood—down and spiraling lower. The student test scores were among the lowest in the district. The mobility rate was among the highest in the district, approximately 60 percent. Student suspensions were high, approximately one hundred the previous year. It was shocking how many students were not advanced to the next grade. They were stuck, and that had to change.

Bear in mind, that was at a time educators could say, "We taught them, but they just did not learn it." Some would call those the good old days, because the responsibility for learning was all on the students. By all indications, very few wanted to be at Tulakes, including parents, students, and teachers.

My first impressions of the school building though were altogether different. Compared to the schools in my previous district, the facilities were outstanding. The school first opened in 1967, which meant it was newer and in better overall condition than almost all the schools I left behind. The halls were wide, well-lit, and carpeted. The rooms were spacious. Lights automatically turned on because of motion detectors when you entered. Windows opened and shut like they were supposed to, and requests for any needed repairs were met with quick responses. This was all new to me, a good kind of new.

Meet the Staff

I was surprised to learn I would have an assistant principal who had once served in the school as a counselor and had applied for the head principal position. This led to a little apprehension on my part. However, after getting to know her, I quickly realized she was one of my greatest and most priceless allies. She was high-character, highly qualified, and she cared about all kids, which is what mattered most to me.

My first encounter with my two administrative assistants was cordial and pleasant. They shared the history, the challenges, and the successes of the school and the community. Unfortunately, the challenges far outweighed the positives.

One moment I will never forget is when one of the administrative assistants asked me to return a parent phone call. I was told in no uncertain terms that the parents were demanding that their child be moved to another class, as they were not going to tolerate their child being the only white child in a classroom full of Blacks. I did not like the implied message, not to mention the fact that moving the child would have resulted in him or her still being only one of two or three Whites in another classroom. I think that may have been one of the only calls I intentionally did not return in my entire career. This was one of many firsts I was to encounter in my new district, but it made me feel good that my office staff found the phone call almost as distasteful as I did.

After a study of the school's recent past, which was less than illustrious, I fastidiously prepared for my first meeting with my new staff. I felt extra conscious of my skin color. I was the only black principal in the district and well aware that many, if not most of the staff were scared to death of their anomalous administrator.

I stood before the teachers with my nice suit, nice cologne, nice shoes, and as nice a smile a guy of my looks could muster. I was very cognizant that first impressions are lasting, and I wanted to "represent." I proceeded with the customary and cursory tasks of introducing myself and sharing about my past, both personally and professionally. My assumption was this would assuage any fears, as my record of serving and service was nothing short of professional, progressive, positive, and personable.

Next, I informed the staff I was there to serve them and the families that entrusted their children to our care. I let them know I had an open-door policy and they should feel free to express their needs and concerns, major or minor. I also shared my vision for the school. I shared that I wanted us to establish a new identity. I shared that I hoped our school would set the bar in every way, from the way our students performed and behaved, to the professional way we looked and professional way we behaved and went about our work.

Every single word out of my mouth was careful and calculated. I enthusiastically expressed that I fully believed in them and what we could and would ultimately achieve working collaboratively. I asked that they join me in having a mindset of optimism and belief that we could turn things around. Most importantly, I urged and exhorted every teacher to seek to build relationships with every student and treat them as though they were their very own biological children. Most of them politely smiled back in tacit agreement, or so I thought. I was optimistic the turnaround was about to begin.

The First Year

To protect the innocent, I will abstain from sharing some of the most disturbing events about that first year, but suffice it to say that neither I nor my message was embraced, at least by many of the staff. However, I will share a few things that happened that I had never witnessed before or even heard about in all of my years of school business.

For example, I had a handful of teachers who sought a transfer in the first couple weeks of school—after the kids had arrived. In my career, I've had teachers who had to resign after the year had begun because of special circumstances such as a spouse getting transferred to another city, but this was entirely different. I had gone out of my way to extend my teachers kindness and support. A handful still decided to transfer or resign. I was taken aback because teachers generally finish what they start. It got so bad that I received a call from the district assistant superintendent over human resources asking if I wanted any additional transfers denied. I kindly asked her to allow anyone that wanted to leave to do so. She eventually did have to deny some transfer requests to prevent disrupting learning substantially.

Another first was to have, more than once, an entire team of five or six teachers in the same grade be absent or leave early on the same day, particularly when data and reports were due. Perhaps it was coincidental, but it seemed an attempt to sabotage my efforts and send me a message.

The students posed different challenges. The culture and climate was such that too many of them had become accustomed to an almost anarchical environment, especially the upper grades. Defiance, opposition, disrespect, fighting, swearing, teasing, and taunting were commonplace, resulting in countless referrals and frustration for some teachers and burnout for others.

Dress was another big issue. In a community of diversity and varied incomes, some students came to school in the latest hip-hop fashion, which had a direct, negative impact on student behavior. Instead of entering the doors of the school with a laser-like focus for gaining knowledge and becoming the best person possible, they were coming to school to "stunt," be cool, dance, and mimic the boisterous and often vulgar behavior of the latest popular hip-hop artists. Our students were buying what the artists were selling, and apparently so was whoever was sending them to school.

The children of families of lesser income were the direct opposite. It was extremely problematic because the children with less were well aware of their economic status. They could compare what they wore with the others. If they somehow failed to notice what they did not have, those with better were more than happy to let them know with no little subtlety. All of this negatively impacted our school. Kids fussed and fought. Children missed school because they and their parents were too ashamed or frustrated to confront this behemoth of an issue.

This brings us to the parents and guardians of our wonderful but extremely vulnerable and impressionable little ones. In many ways, the children were simply repeating the cycle their parents had lived before them. The children were the fruit of the broken education, employment, incarceration, and social systems. Their parents had lived through social storms no less hazardous than some of our state's severest weather.

For some, the violent storms occurred early in life. They were molested, neglected, preyed upon, deceived, and abandoned before they were barely old enough to even know what was happening. For some, the weather took a turn for the worse later, perhaps in high school where their pipeline to prison began. Their schools failed them by not having a safety net. These individuals slammed to ground like Humpty Dumpty never to be put back together again. Some who reached adulthood with a hope of realizing the American Dream were struck down by the cold, hard truth that it would not apply to them. Over time, the weather of life violently ripped every leaf of hope, happiness, and faith from their branches. Over time, all the soil of righteousness, justice, and pride was eroded from their roots and trunks. What was left barely standing was a leafless and barren tree, just tired of being tired.

Our state song, "Oklahoma!," from the popular musical by Rodgers and Hammerstein has a line that says: "We're only sayin' / You're doin' fine, Oklahoma! / Oklahoma, OK." Our families definitely were not doing fine and were anything but OK.

Too many of the parents and guardians of the children were weather-beaten and not hopeful of blossoming or enjoying and affording fruitful or prosperous living. So they sent to school damaged, frail, and unhealthy children who came to school ready to do anything except reading, writing, and arithmetic. Instead, they wanted to fight, rebel, or avoid any type of work in the classroom. They were hungry, tired, angry, sullen. Most of all, they were hurt, but with no vocabulary or space to express their feelings.

The self-image of the school, a direct result of all of the above, was altogether negative. The children, families, and staff should all have been given yearly sympathy cards for withstanding the constant deluge of glares, whispers, and disparaging comments about their school. Many of their harshest critics had never graced the doors of the school. They had no first-hand knowledge of what happened within the walls. We have heard that "sticks and stones may break my bones, but words will never hurt me." But this ditty is absolutely false when it comes to emotional harm, whether to individuals or groups. In fact, and terribly sad, I am aware of numerous incidents where district staff, even in the central administration offices, attempted to dissuade new parents from enrolling their children in Tulakes.

I would be lying if I said the thought of jumping ship never crossed my mind. After all, so many others had. But at the end of the day, I knew Tulakes had to change. I knew the children and families there deserved no less.

Too many leaders act as if the sheep... their people... are there for the benefit of the shepherd, not that the shepherd has responsibility for the sheep.
—Ken Blanchard, author and management consultant

DISCUSSION QUESTIONS FOR CHAPTER THREE

1. How does the author's mindset of positivity and hope influence his leadership and success?

2. How is the role and perspective of the leader important in determining the outcomes for a school?

3. How can you show empathy and understanding for teachers, administrators, and schools whose children and families experience a disproportionate level of hardship and challenges?

4. Do you believe that hope, faith, and a belief that life has purpose are important to a child's development? Why or why not?

5. Have you seen parents and guardians supported in ways that allow them to do their best in nurturing their children? Share some examples.

6. What ideas do you have for better supporting parents who themselves lack needed support?

4

NAVIGATING UNCHARTED TERRITORY

A dream doesn't become reality through magic;
it takes sweat, determination, and hard work.
—General Colin Powell, first African American
Secretary of State and Chair of the Joint Chiefs of Staff

One morning I was sitting in my office, preparing to hopefully awaken and evoke school-wide energy and purpose with the morning announcements, when I suddenly heard a blood-curdling scream followed by shouting in the outer office. I swiftly sprang out my door to encounter a mom spewing dragon-like fire and rage. I got to her just before any horrified staff personnel could call the police. I pleaded and prodded her to step into my office, which she did with great reluctance. She was upset because one of her children phoned and told her a staff member had "grabbed" one of her other children in the cafeteria during breakfast. I am not sure how the child even made the call as this was before cell phones were as common as backpacks, but none-theless a six-foot-something, full-sized woman made her intentions clear that she was on her way to find the staff person, so she could personally "handle the matter just like she had done in another school." Trust me, it was not good. She also boasted that she was under doctor's care to help with her emotions, which made her extra dangerous.

I emphatically told her over and over that I cared about her as a parent, but more importantly I loved all of my students and her children were a part of that all. She still was not buying it. However, what got her attention was when I said if she doubted me, we could call her children into my office and ask them if they thought I loved them. I told her I would even leave when she probed them. It was a gamble, especially with her heightened emotions, but one I was willing to take. I had intentionally been an advocate for our Tulakes kids day in and day out. I just kept repeating it, asking if she would trust me to handle the matter. I encouraged her to check my reputation among other parents if she still did not believe me. After a few minutes, she broke down in tears and shared some personal struggles. I hugged and prayed with and for her, and we never had such a moment again.

Embracing the Parents

As you might imagine, the aforementioned incident was not an aberration at our school. In fact, it was not highly unusual at all. The parent component at Tulakes was an unpredictable, untapped, and undervalued resource. Many well-intentioned institutions had long ago improperly labeled and categorized the guardians, parents, grandparents, and surrogates of our wonderful children. They were unfairly viewed as too busy and inaccessible at best, and uncaring and uninvested at worst.

When I arrived at Tulakes, of our 650 students, maybe ten parents made up the PTA. Only one or two of those were people of color. That small number soon disappeared due to what I would call circumstantial attrition. Having homeroom moms, reliable chaperones for field trips, and parental help in general was sketchy at best. The traditional model of parental involvement and participation was null and void, and I'd submit, not even a worthwhile pursuit. As with most schools of like demographics, if I have heard criticisms of parents once, I have heard them a thousand times. See if you have heard any of these epic presumptions before. Better yet, see if you have thought or uttered any of them.

- "They never show up for anything their child is involved in. They never attend parent teacher conferences to even know how their child is doing. They don't care about their children."
- "Every way possible has been tried to reach the parent(s); calling, texting, emailing, and sending notes, and nothing has worked. That's totally irresponsible."
- "His dad doesn't miss any of his basketball or football games, but he's never once had time to come to the school to talk or visit. He totally has misplaced priorities."
- "She never returns her homework, and the mom doesn't do anything about it. The mom is just lazy."
- "We have scheduled and rescheduled IEPs [Individual Education Plan meetings] for them, but they obviously aren't invested enough. We should report them for child neglect."

I have heard many of these erroneous and unfair comments made firsthand about parents in our public schools. Some teachers apparently had jettisoned from their memory what was learned in college concerning Maslow's Hierarchy of Needs. Simply put, everyone's primary needs must be met first before he or she can attend to secondary or tertiary needs. Who among us could disregard our most basic and immediate needs of food, shelter, safety, and security and still focus on the more distant and intangible issue of our children's education? After all, particularly if education was not the means to an end for you or anyone else in your sphere of influence, how likely would you be to believe it was likely to yield a substantial return for your offspring?

Let's now peel away a few layers of the "parents not involved and don't care" onion. First, let me pause and iterate that I have come to the conclusion that the vast majority of our parents of poverty, especially single moms, are nothing less than miracle workers. Think about it for a minute—working multiple jobs, caring for children at the elementary, middle, and high school levels, perhaps even with younger ones at home, all by yourself, and at no fault of your own. In too many cases, things just happened. A life that possibly started out on a course for the acceptable American quest of "boy meets girl" resulting in "married with children," but cataclysmically resulting in everything but the simple pursuit of happiness. In the words of actress Charlize Theron, "I don't think any mother aims to be a single mom. I didn't wish for that, but it happened."

I have experienced countless parents, mostly single moms, who have lost immediate family members to violence and other tragic and untimely deaths. In fact, a number of them experienced the sudden death of more than one immediate family member. In some cases, the shock alone incapacitated them, not to mention the various actions required of them to deal with the tragedy, from funeral preparation to just coping with the loss, none of which likely involved any form of grief counseling or the most basic help and support.

Another far-too-common and overwhelming issue they faced was incarceration. On more than a couple occasions, I had a mom walk into the office and very calmly and matter-of-factly apologize to an office staff person for not returning a call or the like because she had spent the last few days in jail.

In case you didn't know, the state of Oklahoma incarcerates more women per capita than any other state in the country. Under the same circumstances, most of us would likely burrow ourselves under a rock for an indefinite amount of time, if not something much worse. Unfortunately, a disproportionate number of these mothers had husbands, boyfriends, and children serving sentences at a county, state, or federal lock-up facility, mostly for what I would call "survival offenses." Meanwhile, mom was left "serving time" outside the walls and doing it all by herself. When juxtaposed, it was hard to guess who had it worse —him being behind shiny barbed wire with fellow co-conspirators and gang members or her being locked behind an invisible fence with no one to watch her back. And if the mother is under duress, in all likelihood her children are too. In fact, at one point our school therapist estimated that 85 percent of our children at any given time could potentially be clinically diagnosed with depression.

Moreover, far too many educators aren't the least bit cognizant of their fortuitous existence compared to that of the parents of their students. For most teachers, school is and always has been a haven of sorts. As children, they flourished academically, were teacher favorites, and only visited the principal's office for praise and reward; hence, school was a place they eagerly returned to in adulthood.

However, for some if not many of the guardians of our children, their experiences were polar opposites. Schools, and the people in them, were creepier than any haunted house and arguably some of the most unwelcoming places of all. Imagine if you were being asked back to a place with nightmarish memories of failure upon failure; punishment, even when you did nothing wrong; bullying from students as well as adults. Add to that the fact that the people in the school look, talk, and act in such a way that makes you feel grossly inferior. Most of us would avoid that place like the plague.

As to the complaint of parents' failure to respond to notes, calls, and other messaging, first it's a lofty assumption that any note would arrive in the hands of the intended receiver. Even Beaver Cleaver didn't always do that. Regarding electronic messaging, school personnel far too often underestimate the inaccessibility of phones or computers for some of our parents.

With cell phones, most in the middle class have maintained the same cell phone number for about as long as they can remember. Their numbers have only changed as a matter of prerogative. But for the less fortunate, crises too numerous to count may result in phone services being interrupted time and again. They almost never have the same number from one year to the next. In some cases, they may even have a number change twice in the same month or be without phone service for that same duration.

I should not have to mention Internet access, but I will. Today, in America, I think it is safe to say 99 percent of those in the middle class and up have Internet access within their reach 24-7 if they so desire. Checking social media or email on their phones is the first thing they do in the morning and the last thing they do before bed, so it's inconceivable to be unable to communicate electronically. It rates right up there with oxygen and water. Therefore, it can easily be assumed that everybody has such access at their fingertips. However, for those without expendable income, wifi capability is a luxury and often only available on an intermittent basis.

The issue of dads, especially of low income, attending ball games but failing to show up at school, sounds very legitimate on the surface, but let's not be too hasty to judge. First of all, dads, regardless of income, did not make sports the ubiquitous monster they are today. That guilt is on all of us. Whoever heard of families showing up for school two hours early to tailgate before school starts? Which of our great cities strategically posts pictures of their most prized scholars on skyscrapers or billboards? What academic has ever been pursued relentlessly by the paparazzi? How many autographs of intellectuals have you waited in line to get on a brown paper bag or piece of toilet paper or your bare skin? How many people would know about Lonzo Ball if he were a scientist instead of an NBA player?

In Oklahoma City on July 4, 2016, you would think we had experienced another catastrophe as calamitous as an EF5 tornado or earthquake by the shock and trauma written across people's faces. What had happened instead was that OKC Thunder player Kevin Durant had signed with the Golden State Warriors. A video appeared online of someone burning a No. 35 jersey. Another video showed someone questioning the seven-time All-Star about his heart and manhood. Words like "coward" and "traitor" were used liberally. The news wasn't only local, but also national and even international. No, it is not just low-income dads who place a disquietingly high value on athletic prowess.

In many of our fathers' minds, their sons or daughters are not guaranteed success via the world of academia despite all of dad's best efforts. So dad ends up gambling, placing all his chips on his kid making it to the pros. He bets on athletic fame. Athletes are the people he sees on television all the time. Athletes are the real heroes. Athletes make the big money. Athletes get all the attention. So you tell me, are lower-income dads the exception or the rule? I think they are just like countless others in our country who are closing their eyes, rolling the dice, and praying for lucky number seven. In general, our city, nation, and world value athletics more than education. So I don't think it is only a poor or minority father problem. We shouldn't blame them more than what they deserve for a situation they did not create.

At Tulakes we didn't have many accessible fathers, and most of the ones we had weren't bad guys. They loved their kids just as much as anyone. However, they were coping with overwhelming obstacles. So it looked like they weren't involved at all and looked even worse when their kids weren't doing well in school, but I didn't want to blame the dads. I wanted us to enlist and encourage the ones we had, so we went after them with all we had.

Another issue that frustrates educators is when parents fail to show up for student Individual Educational Planning (IEP) meetings. This is especially important for students who need special education services. As a former special education teacher, I understand the frustration and challenge of trying to schedule and hold these federally mandated meetings. For the special education teacher, amidst your many responsibilities, it can be complicated to schedule with multiple parents meetings that could each last two hours or longer. These meetings require the attendance of a classroom teacher, an administrator, a specialist or two or three, the parent(s), and possibly others. Moreover, if the meeting is held during the day, you still have the responsibility for the instruction of the rest of your students while you are out of the room. The principal also has many responsibilities to juggle as he or she must meet the needs of anyone and everyone as they come while also attending to teacher observations, disciplinary actions, and a host of other meetings.

However, it was not acceptable to demonize parents at our school. We did our best to sympathize and empathize with parents, practice patience, and be creative. Sometimes this meant holding meetings hours before school, like 6 a.m., or hours after school, like 5:30 p.m., and whenever and wherever parents could meet. We just kept trying, even when they had failed to appear numerous times at some of those meetings.

Changing the Tone

In the end, we collectively decided to abandon finger-pointing, accusations, and excuses. We decided to take matters into our own hands. One of the first things we did to change the culture was to host an evening meal and dance at the school for our families. We brought in a local professional hip-hop band, and we served a meal from a popular local restaurant. The staff danced and ate with students and parents. The parents were blown away as the mostly non-black staff boogied and did the Bus Stop, Electric Slide, Cha Cha, and Macarena with them well into the night. I loved the look in their eyes. They were just astounded that there was no other agenda except to have fun and transform a negative mindset of the school being an unwelcoming, unfriendly, and scary place for parents to just the opposite. We wanted them to "Celebrate Good Times, Come On!" It was the beginning of something great.

Shortly after the dance party, we decided to rethink how we pursued the matter of parent involvement. Without consciously or audibly invoking it, we collectively adopted the Serenity Prayer: God, grant me the serenity to accept the things I cannot change, courage to change the things I can, and wisdom to know the difference.

After much thought, we conceded that we did not necessarily

need our parents to be involved in traditional ways. As noted before, they had bigger issues to contend with, and that was just a fact. So we took a thorough look at our calendar. We listed and reviewed all the events that parents were most likely to participate in or attend. We then decided to capitalize on and maximize relationships, partnering, and student support at each of those occasions. After a careful analysis, we listed the events where we could get the biggest bang for our buck. They included: Back to School Bash, Parent Orientation, Open House, Donuts for Dads, Muffins for Moms, Daddy Daughter Dance, Black History Month Celebration, International Day, Student Promotion, and Pre-K enrollment.

Back to School Bash

Our Back to School Bash set the tone for the year. It was like the party previously mentioned. Knowing full well that every year many of our parents were new to the neighborhood, we were aware of the lingering negative perceptions of the school and community. So we took advantage of the beginning-of-the-year parent anxiety, anticipation, and excitement to meet and engage them, and to love on their children. We wanted to make a statement that this was *their school*. We were there to serve them well.

We held this event in front of the school to make it impossible for any parent passing by to miss and for any child to dismiss. We advertised it on the school marquee, and we made follow-up phone calls by the teachers and an automated call from me, the principal.

Then with the support of community partners, we always provided food, fun, and more. Who could turn down a free burger or hotdog, chips, and a drink on a hot August afternoon? We also offered moon bounces, face painting, games, door prizes, and sometimes wrap-around services and information like free dental checkups, eye exams, counseling resources, and other family services. This event was always a hit, and at its conclusion each year I am not sure who looked upon the oncoming year with more excitement, the parent, the child, or the staff. Thus, our first goal of generating excitement and making a good first impression was accomplished.

Parent Orientation and Open House

Parent Orientation and Open House was our next strategic event. We were well aware that many of our parents dreaded this night. Parents did not want to sit only to be deluged with excessive information. The staff didn't want this either. So we decided to make the evening more rewarding and enjoyable for everyone. We were determined that this event wouldn't be merely perfunctory, but a time parents could really become empowered to help their children be successful.

We shared basics on policy and procedures regarding homework, attendance, and curriculum, but our teachers went much further. They outlined grade-specific services, opportunities, resources, and strategies that, if heeded, would almost guarantee success for each and every student. Perhaps the most consistently beneficial information was that the teachers shared their personal cell phone numbers, which the parents were free to call any time of day. We wanted them to be able to reach us, and we vowed to take their calls.

We begged our parents to take advantage of before- and after-school tutoring or help when offered. We informed the parents that almost all staff arrived at least an hour before school or stayed at least an hour after school ended. We were more than willing to provide additional time and instruction. We knew some of the parents were (for any number of reasons) unable to assist students with homework, so the teachers took it upon themselves to assist them. Some, on their own volition, even picked up children and took them home afterwards. It took more time and commitment, but we viewed it as a win-win-win situation. The children would prosper from the expert assistance, and the teachers would reap the spoils of having a great relationship and partnership with both parent and child. The parents' minds were blown away at the support, friendship, partnership, and love they experienced.

Donuts for Dads

Donuts for Dads and Mornings for Moms were some of the favorite and most anticipated events of the year. These yielded immeasurably positive results. Prior to my arrival, these events had been come-and-go events where moms and dads made obligatory stops by the school before going to work. They popped in, had juice and a pastry, took a photograph with their child, and left. Sometimes the parent was never seen again for the remainder of the year. Some thought they had done their duty, or just didn't know what to do, or both. However, that was about to change.

The staff and I concluded that we were missing out on a grand opportunity if we failed to connect with dads and other men who had relationships with our kids at Tulakes. If we could only get some of the men, be it dads, estranged or not, big brothers, uncles, grandpas, or boyfriends of moms, into our school once a year, why not make the most of the opportunity? We knew we only had one chance to make a first impression.

We decided to change this annual event from a drive-by (in and out) to a drive-into (come and partake). We made a program involving the top student essays about the important man in their lives and why he was picked as such. These essays were terribly moving and impactful—out of the mouths of babes. We had special music, often from our choir, which sounded to me like the famous Hallelujah Chorus. We featured a testimonial from a father who had overcome formidable odds to be and remain present and viable in the lives of his children.

One dad in particular was a single father of six. Women do it all the time, but he was truly an exception in our world, if not the world over. As a man, he refused to abdicate his responsibility by abandoning his children or seeking a maternal figure for the wrong reason. He passionately shared how he worked, cooked, washed, cleaned, attended games, helped with homework, disciplined, and did everything else by himself. It was awe inspiring. The other fathers and I gave him a raving ovation.

These short speeches were always powerful for the other men in attendance. They could see someone they knew and could relate to, which helped eliminate their excuses. I always followed with a short, inspirational message, consisting of statistics and other important information. I ended with a passionate charge to, in the words of the late NCAA coach Jim Valvano, "Never give up. No matter what, never ever give up!"

We knew too many of the men had left the "school biz" and such up to females, and they probably did not know much more beyond just saying to the children, "Get a good education." We resolved to do more. We wanted to inspire active participation and encourage anyone who made that valiant attempt. We provided them with practical, hands-on methods to get and stay involved (see Resources at the end of the book).

Each year, our crowds grew larger and larger, as men responded in ways that were both gratifying and encouraging to the staff, but most importantly to our beloved children. We knew not every heart was pricked to action, but if only one father heeded the challenge, then time was well spent.

Mornings for Moms

Mornings for Moms was formatted much the same as the dads event. It was dedicated to the mothers or special women in the lives of our children. As I mentioned earlier, a disproportionate number of our students had no father figure. Thus, our moms were often trying to parent all by themselves.

As with the men, we wanted to capitalize on the mothers' presence by encouraging and equipping them. We recognized that many of their plates were full, and helping their children with school work was often formidable for some and impossible for others. We provided specific and simple means to do so. We encouraged the moms that they should allow their children to either call the teacher or come early to school if possible to get any needed assistance.

This event was always well attended. Any and every mother who possibly could was always present to represent her child or children, which is why we deservedly celebrate and esteem mothers as we do. For our program each year, I sought out and secured a mom to speak, one who could say "I started from the bottom, but now I'm here." I was blessed each year to find a mother with a powerful and tantalizing testimonial to share with the other mothers.

One mother in particular shared how she grew up in the area and wrestled with the monstrous challenges that poverty can present. As a result of sexual abuse and ultimately premature and unprotected sexual involvement, she eventually had a child at age fifteen, putting her high school completion and graduation in jeopardy. But she defied the odds, ultimately graduating from an alternative high school. She went on to attain a college degree. She is now working with moms to do the same. After she told her story, she received resounding applause with very few dry eyes in the room. I simply could not have written a better script. They got the message that if the speaker could do it, so could they. I ended the program by lifting up the moms with a brief sermonette and proclaiming, "Yes you can! Yes, you can! Yes, you can!"

Daddy Daughter Dance

The Daddy Daughter Dance was a special event we added my last year at Tulakes, but not without some last-minute drama and adjustments. On the eve of the dance, at an event away from our school, I ran into one of my little girls. She said, "Mr. Roland, I can't go to the Daddy Daughter Dance tomorrow night." I asked her why not, as we had tried to eliminate every possible reason by allowing fathers, uncles, grandpas, neighbors, or friends to accompany them. She sadly informed me that she had no dad or male in her life to accompany her. She reiterated that she had no one. No one.

I was heartbroken. It was not OK that this beautiful and innocent little girl would be left out because life had already left her without. I knew that life was not fair and not everybody gets to have what everybody else has. However, I did not want my school to contribute to any of the unfairness or cruelty of life. So the next morning, I got on the PA system and made an urgent announcement: "Any and every girl who wishes to attend the Daddy Daughter Dance is welcome to come tonight." I subsequently called almost every man I knew, as well as our church partners, and told them to dress up and be at our school early that evening. I told them they were needed to be surrogate dads.

When it was all said and done, some of the men, including

me, had a host of daughters that evening, and we danced the night away. It made my day to make those girls' nights.

I wanted to end the night with the girls leaving inspired, so we had them repeat after me as loudly as they could the Tulakes Girls Affirmations:

- I have no right to compare myself to anyone. Why? Because, I am fearfully and wonderfully made!
- I strive only to be MY highest self. There is NO limit to what I can do!
- I choose to see the light that I am to this world. I am a candle in the dark of night!
- I will never settle in life. I am the best! I want the best! And I will only accept the best!
- I see myself as a gift to others, to my family, to my community, to my country, and to the world. I am slowly being unwrapped, but I am a gift!

It was a good night. I was happy. The volunteers were happy. And most importantly, a bunch of little girls were happy.

Black History Month

Our Black History Month celebrations were second to none and I believe were one of the most significant holidays we recognized. One group at the school was learning to love, accept, and appreciate the other. Those on the other side were learning to love, accept, and appreciate themselves. Both types of learning were life-changing.

Before I arrived at Tulakes, there was no recognition of black history or the contributions of Blacks in America. I suggested we correct that omission. Some of the staff really bought in and totally championed this opportunity. Others went along for the ride at first, but eventually became drivers of this celebration. In some cases, non-black staff, children, and parents experienced a metamorphosis of sorts. They moved from apathy and blindness to empathy and awareness. Their black history education, I assert, is one the most transformative movements in our school's turnaround.

In the words of Robert Noyce, technologist and entrepreneur: "Knowledge is power. Knowledge shared is power multiplied." I was intentional in encouraging the staff to embrace this concept, which thankfully they did. A cross-racial committee worked to maximize our efforts to impact our children.

So how did we celebrate Black History Month? Our recognition lasted the entire month of February and sometimes even beyond. Each day of the month our announcements included a black history trivia question or special moment in black history. Children and staff of every color had fun researching and discovering the history of African Americans. With the help of staff and community, our amazing media specialist converted the library into an interactive museum of sorts with relics, books, and more.

Not only were our children educated, enlightened, and inspired, but so were the faculty. In fact, the staff was sometimes even more surprised than the kids by some of the facts. Our children were encouraged and inspired to think beyond their micro-circumstances to macro-possibilities. They were encouraged to have a dream in the vein of the great Dr. Martin Luther King Jr.

The celebration created an atmosphere of unity amidst a school of diversity. In a country and world where divisiveness and hatred are rampant (evidenced in our nation's capital; Charleston, South Carolina; Ferguson, Missouri; Charlottesville, Virginia; the Black Lives Matter movement; Confederate symbols; kneeling or not during the National Anthem), we acknowledged past wrongs but also highlighted incredible achievements of African Americans. This moved us toward unity and oneness.

Our staff and families learned about a culture that was maligned, misunderstood, misrepresented, and unfamiliar to many of them, largely as a result of what was ironically not taught to them in a place called school. So we taught them, just much later. The ultimate beneficiaries were our wonderful students and families.

Second, and more important, the Black History Month celebrations were priceless for our black students and their families. This cannot be overstated. I believe the greatest enemy of many of our black children is a lack of self-love. Malcolm X said that discrimination resulted in Black self-hatred, manifested in hair-straightening, the love of anything non-Black, the proliferation of crime, drug addiction, alcoholism, and other negative behaviors. As a result of our nation's painful history of enslavement and Jim Crow laws and the influence of media and hip-hop, far too many of our nation's black youths have accepted a status of second classism, "I can't-ism," and worst of all, "I'm not-ism."

Our celebrations helped our black students see themselves in an entirely new light. Instead of viewing their history as beginning in slavery and savagery, they looked back further to Africa and discovered they were kings, queens, master builders and carpenters, physicians, mathematicians, scientists, artists, discoverers, farmers, and more. Instead of viewing themselves as weaklings, they discovered that they were the offspring of regal strength. Instead of thinking they made little to no contributions to this country, they learned that they built the mansions of their masters and other great architectural wonders. Their people were inventors, pioneers, innovators, writers, speakers, designers, culinary geniuses, beauticians, and more, much of which they never were given credit or recognition for by historians.

Instead of believing they could only aspire to do something with a ball, be an entertainer, or be a kingpin of illicit activity, they could have aspirations in politics, medicine, education, architecture, the arts, business, and more. Instead of believing that Black is ugly and bad, they learned that Black is beautiful and good if they want it to be and let it be!

Part of our celebration included an "I Have a Dream" coloring contest for our youngest and pre-writing students. Our older children were tasked to submit an "I Have a Dream" essay. Their essays could be about tolerance and unity, or they could be about a dream they had for themselves, which we encouraged and preferred. The best were submitted to a judging committee that awarded prizes. We believed students would ultimately better be able to "love thy neighbor" if they honed in on a dream to be the best person they could be and put that dream in writing as a constant reminder. I hope each child will continue to clutch tightly to his or her dream, with educators doing everything possible to usher those dreams to fruition.

The highlight of our celebration was our Black History Program, where our planning committee put on a major drama and music program. To capture as many viewers as possible, we generally held two programs, one during the day and another at night. We invited central office administrators, community partners, and parents to come see us show off. And show off we did!

Some of our activities included talents and messages from African American kings and queens, fraternity and sorority stompers from our local Historical Black University, Langston University, and high school and civic leaders in our cities. The highlight was always our very own students who performed skits and enactments that were jaw-dropping. Most of the time, our events ended in rousing ovations and tears. This event became a signature statement of our commitment to educate some, eradicate the ignorance of some, emancipate some, and encourage everyone to be the change they hoped to see.

The Black History Month celebrations played a key role in our efforts to promote positive behavior in our predominantly black student population. Again, since many of our black youths have difficulty loving themselves, are hopeless, or both, the result is frequently inappropriate school behavior, lack of academic success, and eventually more harmful consequences—gang affiliation, unplanned pregnancies, dropping out of school, or the pipeline to prison. Schools need to be intentional about addressing this lack of proper self-love and hope.

Promotion Program

An end-of-year Promotion Program was our last special event of the year and was important for garnering the attention and affection of the parents of our youngest and oldest students, PreK and fifth grade. We took full advantage of these two opportunities to promote parent involvement and school pride.

The parents and relatives of our youngest students, PreK and kindergarten, were the most anxious and eager to attend special events like Open House, field trips, Christmas parties, and Valentine's Day parties. To capitalize on their parental involvement, I made it a priority to take advantage of their zeal by demonstrating my commitment to them and their children's education, and in the process, gain their support.

When parents, grandparents, and other relatives filed into our facility, there were often standing-room-only crowds. I would first bellow, "I love you!" and then tell them how appreciative I was that they entrusted their legacies to me and the Tulakes' staff.

Then I would tell them about the good things going on at our school such as minimum discipline problems, rising test scores, and the best staff this side of heaven with minimal staff turnover, which was vital information for them to know and hopefully spread. I knew the importance of parent retention (keeping children stable and our school from being a musical chairs of sorts) and that word of mouth was key.

I used this opportunity to ask parents and guardians to partner with us in educating their wonderful students. I articulated how important summers were for our children. Summers were a time to stop the ice cream truck in the street, go swimming, and take vacations if they could. But summers were also a time where our children needed to keep learning. I urged them to take home summer packets from teachers and visit libraries. I slipped in other general parenting suggestions to help them help their children. Our end-of-year programs gave us invaluable advertisement and support that money cannot buy—word of mouth through positive engagement from the parents of our children. Overall, our efforts and strategy paid off with great dividends.

Parent One-on-Ones

By far, the most effective parent-behavior-altering method I employed though was one-on-one parent conversations. I worked on changing parent behavior by showing my heart and character.

For most, taking care of our young is almost a primal instinct. I understood and respected that, especially for some of our single moms, who in too many cases had nothing but their children for companionship and support. They wanted success for their kids, even when they hadn't experienced it themselves. Therefore, especially when a parent was upset, I would frequently come from behind my desk and take a seat next to the parent, look him or her in the eyes and listen intently. Sometimes, I would even remove my tie and sit on the floor. I made every effort to help them understand that I did not think that I was above them, standing in judgment or condemnation, or in any way devoid of sensitivity. However long it took, I would convey and convince them that I loved their children and had worked tirelessly to recruit a staff team that felt the same. I assured them as best I could that any wrong would be made right.

For the most part, they left convinced, because I meant every word I said.

The only way to do great work is to love what you do.
—Steve Jobs, inventor and entrepreneur

DISCUSSION QUESTIONS FOR CHAPTER FOUR

1. What is your response to the negative statements about parents and guardians? Have you ever experienced positive belief about someone resulting in a better positive outcome?
2. What experiences have you had with parents and guardians who have a lack of communication tools? Whose responsibility is it to facilitate healthy and consistent communication?
3. What school programs mentioned in this chapter stand out to you and why?
4. What do you know about the history of Blacks in Africa? What are your thoughts on the author's comments that "one group was learning to love, accept, and appreciate the other, while those on the other side were learning to love, accept, and appreciate themselves"?
5. What value to do you see in providing practical,

hands-on methods for parents and guardians to be and stay involved?

6. Why do you think it is important that parents and guardians know you love their children and will work hard to see them succeed?

BOOSTING PASSENGER MORALE AND BEHAVIOR

I am bright; there is nothing I cannot do.
Yesterday's failures are behind me,
Tomorrow's successes are yet before me,
And I will make today the very best day of all,
For this day begins the rest of my life.
I will aid my teacher in every way possible
To ensure that my life is on the right track.
I realize that if I want to succeed
That the first step must truly be my own.
—Tulakes Creed

When I arrived at Tulakes, student "misbehavior" was the issue everybody talked about. I was quickly told of a fifth grader from the year before who seemingly lacked the most basic social skills. I was told that on one occasion, when he returned to his classroom after a bathroom break and found the door locked, he knocked loudly and said, "Hey, open this f%@#ing door." When approached and questioned by his teacher, he apparently had no idea he had said anything wrong.

Well, I am from the old school, and a Black old school at that. In my day, parents said things like: "I brought you in this world and I'll take you out," "A hard head makes for a soft behind," "This whipping is gonna hurt me worse than it hurts you," and "Some people don't believe fat meat is greasy until it's hot." I did not understand some of those aphorisms as a child, but I got the general idea: children were to be subjective to people in authority or else. We were not given suggestions or requests, but rather directives and ultimatums. Therefore, my expectations for children have always been extremely high.

However, that does not mean I am a proponent of severe punishment, physical (corporal) or non-physical (suspension/expulsion), across the board. For instance, I don't believe corporal punishment should ever occur without parental consent, and I don't think suspension or expulsion should be applied unless there is extremely inappropriate behavior. Such behavior would include violence, serious sexual misconduct, and significant defiance of authority (of those who are first fair and respectful of students). I also think school leaders should take into consideration how a suspension would affect the parent's employment, though I know this is not a popular idea. But for those with low-wage jobs, missing work can easily result in termination, which only exacerbates the situation for the child in the long run.

So, high expectations yes, but mixed with understanding.

Expectations Assembly

To make those expectations crystal clear, we held a school-wide Expectations Assembly the first or second week of school. We usually waited five to seven days to allow students to settle in just a bit and to allow time for late enrollees to show up. The objective of this assembly was to share what I as the principal expected of the student body. My presentation with visuals accommodated all ages and learning styles. I detailed what was expected, as well as the consequences if those expectations were not met.

I aimed to provide both awareness and caution for most, and perhaps an element of fear for others. I wanted students to act appropriately so teachers could teach and learners could learn. This assembly set the tone to help us accomplish these goals.

Classroom Walk-Throughs

Administrators and counselors also made daily classroom walk-throughs. These were invaluable for influencing positive student behavior. We observed instructional and management practices that directly impacted student behavior, and we provided feedback (positive and corrective) as warranted. We wanted to ensure students were being engaged and monitored, highlighting best practices in every class.

Students were well aware I or another designee might walk into their classroom at any time. Sometimes teachers discreetly, or not, made us aware of students who needed special affirmation or attention so we could give them a wink, light touch on the shoulder, or some brief counsel before we exited. Students knew that getting "caught in the act" was not a good thing, especially by me. Also, because of the rapport I and other school leaders had built with them, they knew they were loved and didn't want to let us down. Sometimes, I purposely went in and out of the room several times or stayed much longer than usual just to let a student know he or she had my attention, if you know what I mean. The visits were helpful in maintaining an atmosphere conducive to learning.

The Effort Grade

We also implemented a school-wide incentive plan known as the Effort Grade, which paid huge dividends in promoting self-discipline and positive behavior (see Resources). My leadership team and I decided we would take the novel approach of consistently rewarding *good* behavior instead of only correcting bad behavior. It would be like an auto insurance company rewarding you for being a good driver.

We created a rubric with student input, involving work effort, following expectations inside and outside the classroom, and other behaviors, on a scale of one to three (with three as the highest). We explained the system to parents. We gave each student a grade every day, and we communicated the grades to parents. It was an easy way to keep them informed and also to gain their alliance.

The students were awarded quarterly for earning a certain percentage of threes. It was like an Olympic diver or skater accumulating points and being awarded a gold, silver, or bronze medal. Quarterly awards included pizza parties, bounce houses, dances, extra recesses, and ice cream. Students quickly became motivated to do the right thing! My heart swelled when I encountered students, especially those who struggled with making good choices, breathless and overflowing with joy and pride for earning a three. For some of them it was like winning the lottery but better, because they earned it and had control of their winning and losing.

Since the Effort Grade was assigned at the end of each day, it provided daily feedback. It was something that did not differentiate students by ability, but rather by choices. Every student could succeed. The Effort Grade was helpful both for students who were intrinsically motivated and those who were extrinsically motivated. It was a win-win for our school.

Report Cards

At least quarterly, some of our lowest performing students got an opportunity for some "principal time." These weighty meetings were held with students who were failing or performing well below their abilities. During our time, I would probe them as to the reason for their lack of performance. I was very serious and helped them to feel likewise. I inquired if their grades were due to issues at school (their teacher's instruction, peer distraction, or the like) or things at home (feeling unsafe, lacking basic needs, and the like) or, or, or just a lack of effort. I assured them if it were school or home related that I would exhaust every effort to ameliorate the situation. However, if it was their lack of focus, I expected them to in no uncertain terms exhaust every effort to fix the matter themselves. Happily, I often did not see the same students from one quarter to the next. I had similar meetings with struggling students prior to testing. It was amazing how many ideas we came up with together to help them reach their goals.

High-Flyer List

The High-Flyer List (also called the Behavior Safety Net, see Resources) was another effective tool in changing behaviors. Originally, the list consisted of the top ten Most Wanted (challenging) students in the school. It was later renamed for political correctness and modified to include any student in significant need of intervention based on teacher feedback, office referrals, or counselor involvement and input.

To put it gently, these were students in need of chronic intervention. Many of them would likely have qualified for special education or intensive assistance from a mental health professional. They stretched even the most patient, talented, and experienced teachers. But we created a safety net for them. Their names were highlighted in red on a list we monitored and discussed each month. Through our care and intervention, our goal was to advance the students to at least yellow (being monitored) and ideally to green (no longer in need of extra support).

Our intervention included home visits, counseling, rewards, consequences, and classroom changes. I just prayed for some, though that was not an official part of our intervention. You might say no stone was left unturned. Thankfully, through our individual and concerted efforts, we were able to move almost every one of these students off the High-Flyer List or at least mitigate behavior to a tolerable level.

Annual Girls Retreat

Our Annual Girls Retreat provided a significant boost to our female students. After attending an event on human trafficking, one of our staff approached me with the idea of having a girls sleepover. She wanted to recruit as many volunteer role models as possible for an evening to fill our girls with self-love, dignity, and pride. And to have fun!

Most of the female staff forfeited an entire night's rest to participate in this event. Volunteers also were recruited from churches, universities, and the community. Of course I did not stay, but I attended the opening session and encouraged all the girls before I left.

The evening included a special, formal-style dinner and a program that included videos and guest speakers. However, mostly, the ladies and girls just did things that ladies and girls like to do, such as painting fingernails, combing hair, and talking—lots of talking.

I knew our first event had been a success by what I encountered the morning after. When I arrived at the school, I found a sponsor walking with a sobbing fourth grade girl. The reason she was crying was because she did not want the event to end. She'd had the time of her life! That made *me* want to cry.

Boys to Men Event

Not to be outdone, our Boys to Men Event was just as huge. My male staff and I wanted an evening to pour into our boys. We recruited the help of men from area churches and others in the community. We wanted all of the boys to attend, but were extra intentional in encouraging the boys we knew *needed* to attend.

At Tulakes we wanted our boys to know the value of education and effort. We wanted our boys to know how to treat females. We wanted our boys to know how to set goals. We wanted our boys to know how to be leaders and not followers. We wanted the boys to know about being knocked down, but how to get back up. We wanted the boys to know about some of our mistakes and failures. We wanted our boys to enjoy an evening of hanging around positive males and to just have fun!

The evening included a manly, informal-style meal. Our program included videos and guest speakers. However, mostly the men and boys just did things that men and boys like to do, such as playing basketball, video, and other games, and talking— lots of talking.

I'll never forget talking with one of the teachers who transported a carload of boys home after our first event. She asked the boys if they had a good time. They responded resoundingly that they had a *great* time. She asked them what was the best part of the evening. Bear in mind that we had food, fun, and games—all the things guys love to do. To her utter disbelief, to a person, they each said what they enjoyed most was just hearing about the men's families and homes. It was just a ho-hum world that the other men and I took for granted (living in a home, cutting the grass, washing the car, eating dinner together, going to church together, etc.), but one that was totally unfamiliar to those boys. I wanted to cry.

An article by Phillip Jackson, Executive Director of the Black Star Project in Chicago, so well states the dilemma I wanted our staff to first understand and then address that I want to include it here in full. In "America Has Lost a Generation of Black Boys," Jackson says:

There is no longer a need for dire predictions, hand-wringing, or apprehension about losing a generation of black boys. It is too late. In education, employment, economics, incarceration, health, housing, and parenting, we have lost a generation of young black men. The question that remains is will we lose the next two or three generations, or possibly every generation of black boys hereafter to the streets, negative media, gangs, drugs, poor education, unemployment, father absence, crime, violence, and death.

Most young black men in the United States don't graduate from high school. Only 35% of black male students graduated from high school in Chicago and only 26% in New York City, according to a 2006 report by The Schott Foundation for Public Education. Only a few black boys who finish high school actually attend college, and of those few black boys who enter college, nationally, only 22% of them finish college.

Young black male students have the worst grades, the lowest test scores, and the highest dropout rates of all students in the country. When these young black men don't succeed in school, they are much more likely to succeed in the nation's criminal justice and penitentiary system. And it was discovered recently that even when a young black man graduates from a U.S. college, there is a good chance that he is from Africa, the Caribbean or Europe, and not the United States.

Black men in prison in America have become as American as apple pie. There are more black men in prisons and jails in the United States (about 1.1 million) than there are black men incarcerated in the rest of the world combined. This criminalization process now starts in elementary schools with black male children as young as six and seven years old being arrested in staggering numbers according to a 2005 report, Education on Lockdown by the Advancement Project.

The rest of the world is watching and following the lead of America. Other countries including England, Canada, Jamaica, Brazil and South Africa are adopting American social policies that encourage the incarceration and destruction of young black men. This is leading to a worldwide catastrophe. But still, there is no adequate response from the American or global black community.

Worst of all is the passivity, neglect and disengagement of the black community concerning the future of our black boys. We do little while the future lives of black boys are being destroyed in record numbers. The schools that black boys attend prepare them with skills that will make them obsolete before, and if, they graduate. In a strange and perverse way, the black community, itself, has started to wage a kind of war against young black men and has become part of this destructive process.

Who are young black women going to marry? Who is going to build and maintain the economies of black communities? Who is going to anchor strong families in the black community? Who will young black boys emulate as they grow into men? Where is the outrage of the black community at the destruction of its black boys? Where are the plans and the supportive actions to change this? Is this the beginning of the end of the black people in America?

The list of those who have failed young black men includes our government, our foundations, our schools, our media, our black churches, our black leaders, and even our parents. Ironically, experts say that the solutions to the problems of young black men are simple and relatively inexpensive, but they may not be easy, practical or popular. It is not that we lack solutions as much as it is that we lack the will to implement these solutions to save black boys. It seems that government is willing to pay billions of dollars to lock up young black men, rather than the millions it would take to prepare them to become viable contributors and valued members of our society.

Please consider these simple goals that can lead to solutions for fixing the problems of young black men:

Short term

1) Teach all black boys to read at grade level by the third grade and to embrace education.

2) Provide positive role models for black boys.

3) Create a stable home environment for black boys that includes contact with their fathers.

4) Ensure that black boys have a strong spiritual base.

5) Control the negative media influences on black boys.

6) Teach black boys to respect all girls and women.

Long term

1) Invest as much money in educating black boys as in locking up black men.

2) Help connect black boys to a positive vision of themselves in the future.

3) Create high expectations and help black boys live into those high expectations.

4) Build a positive peer culture for black boys.

5) Teach black boys self-discipline, culture and history.

6) Teach black boys and the communities in which they live to embrace education and life-long learning.[5]

*I don't necessarily have to like my players and associates,
but as their leader I must love them. Love is loyalty,
love is teamwork, love respects the dignity of the individual.
This is the strength of any organization.*
—Vince Lombardi, football coach and NFL executive

DISCUSSION QUESTIONS FOR CHAPTER FIVE

1. Reread the Tulakes Creed. Do you like this creed? Why or why not?
2. What do you think of taking into consideration how consequences like suspensions might impact parents?
3. Describe the value that recognizing students by their choices rather than abilities might create.
4. Why is it important to create an environment where every child feels like he or she can be a success?
5. How does it make you feel that the worlds of children of poverty can differ so substantially from those of middle class?
6. How can you change the realities and outcomes for African-American boys with whom you work?

NO ROOM FOR STOWAWAYS

*Executives owe it to the organization and to their fellow workers
not to tolerate nonperforming individuals in important jobs.*
—Peter Drucker, author and management consultant

"Mr. Roland, our school always has been and likely always will
be the most-challenged and lowest-performing school in the
district. It is just a reality of this community and all the issues that
they have." Thus said a *former* Tulakes Elementary teacher.

A great crew is essential for any successful voyage! No voyage
is going to be smooth sailing all the way; storms are inevitable.
Therefore, fastidious attention must be paid to the character and
competence of the crew. In order for Tulakes to experience a
renaissance of any kind, the crew needed a paradigm shift.

Office Staff

When I was appointed principal, the office staff and administration were the first to receive my intentionality and vision. We reported to school in August two weeks before the teachers, so I worked toward establishing camaraderie. After I took them to lunch, I gently informed them that I expected challenges and issues outside of the office from time to time since those were an inherent part of our work. However, inside the office, I expected minimum conflict. My expectation was for us to be united in serving the staff, our children, and their families.

I reminded them to anticipate calls and visits from upset and anxious students, parents, and staff. Yet we needed to be prepared to respond to them with courtesy, professionalism, and positivity. We ended up working well together, averting many issues that can morph into gargantuan ones when not anticipated in advance. This front-end intentionality paid huge dividends down the road.

Teaching Staff

I next turned my attention to the teaching staff, clearly the most vital members of our crew. The staff I inherited was like many in our urban cities. Their demographic makeup was almost completely opposite that of the population they served. They were middle-class, white female teachers working with lower-income children of color. As is the case across our nation, there was a tremendous cultural divide between these entities. One study states:

> In the fall of 2011, the Center for American Progress released an issue brief looking at teacher diversity, and the findings

were stark. We found that the demographics of the teacher workforce had not kept up with student demographics. In that study, we showed that students of color made up more than 40 percent of the school-age population. In contrast, teachers of color were only 17 percent of the teaching force.[6]

At the beginning of my tenure as principal at Tulakes, I intentionally resisted making too many radical changes beyond visiting classes daily and requiring weekly lesson plans (which were more radical than I thought because both were surprisingly viewed as insults by my staff). Otherwise, I did as little as possible to rock the boat. However, I could hardly wait for year two so I could really begin trying to recreate a radically different and healthier school culture.

One of our first professional development sessions in year two centered around Ruby Payne's book *A Framework for Understanding Poverty*. It was eye-opening for many of our staff to compare the disparate existence of the upper, middle, and lower classes. For as unfamiliar as they were with the world of generational wealth, they were exponentially oblivious to the unnerving and bane world of generational poverty.

They learned about "casual" versus "formal" register, how people in the various classes speak. They learned about definitions and resources. They learned the economics and spending habits of the various classes. They learned the "hidden rules" and routines among classes. For example, Payne writes:

> Being able physically to fight or have someone who is willing to fight for you is important to survival in poverty. Yet, in middle class, being able to use words as tools to negotiate conflict is crucial. Many times the fists are used in poverty because the words are neither available nor respected.[7]

Yet even as the staff read and discussed these insights, I wondered whether they would retain mere head knowledge. I had some incredulity whether the teachers were making the connections from the text to the real-life situations of our students.

In our discussions, some staff felt they had a good grasp on the issues that faced the poor, especially if their own families had been poor in recent decades. They talked about how they (or their parents) had worked hard to pull themselves up by their bootstraps. In their minds, anyone could do the same. If they didn't, they drew conclusions ranging from being misguided and lazy to lacking intellectual adroitness.

However, I had two cautions.

First, I urged them not to compare today's poverty to yesterday's poverty. There is no comparison! Our society was a lot healthier thirty, twenty, or even ten years ago. People once did not lock their doors because it wasn't necessary. Drug and alcohol abuse was not at epidemic proportions. Incarceration was not at outrageous proportions.

Our level of comfort and wealth today is a relatively recent American phenomenon. In times past, most middle-class Americans had and spent less than today. A family of four living in a three-thousand-plus square foot house, with bedrooms and bathrooms for each person, and an extra living and dining room is a relatively new thing. Everyone in a household above age sixteen having a car is a relatively new thing. Spending thousands of dollars on dental or vision care, particularly for cosmetic purposes, is a relatively new thing. Having the latest tech gadget, just because, is a relatively new thing. Having to own name-brand athletic shoes and clothing is a relatively new thing. Dining out multiple times in one week is a relatively new thing.

Additionally, the extended family really was extended and

thus readily available for emotional and practical support. Not having that support is a relatively new thing, and nobody has suffered more than the poor. The gap today between the haves and have-nots is wider, and thus more catastrophic.

Second, the chances of someone escaping the clutches of poverty are tougher today than they have ever been. It's more difficult now to ascend from the lower to the middle class. The poor are incarcerated at a higher rate. The poor receive the highest interest rates. The poor eat more poorly. The poor are fined for failure to pay fines. The poor are penalized if they become a little less poor. For example, an increase in pay of as little as a dime per hour can result in assistance going away. The poor can be denied employment for poor credit scores. The poor have poor access to quality health care, physical or mental. The poor are more likely to be penalized by negative background checks and possibly never to be given a second chance.

As Sal Albanese, a former inner-city teacher, writes:

> During my eleven years as a New York City public school teacher, I saw firsthand the impact that poverty has on the classroom. In low-income neighborhoods like Sunset Park, where I taught, students as young as five years old enter school affected by the stresses often created by poverty: domestic violence, drug abuse, gang activity.[8]

By the end of our discussions of *A Framework for Understanding Poverty*, our staff had better head knowledge regarding the plight of the poor, which was at least a start. However, I wanted them to move toward also having heart knowledge that would move them toward transformative teaching.

"After the Doors Close" Presentation

The second semester of year two, I created a staff development presentation titled "After the Doors Close: Teacher Attitude and Its Impact on Student Achievement." This was my first direct effort to address the multifaceted issues of culture, race, discrimination, opportunity, and the lack thereof in America, especially with regard to its manifestation in our public schools.

The presentation exposed realities about the worlds of Blacks and Whites that far too many of us don't know or know but are reticent to discuss. Whites will talk about it with other Whites. Blacks will talk about it with other Blacks. But we do not want to discuss it across racial lines, other than on social media which more often serves to fan the flames rather than put out the fires. We certainly do not talk about it in schools and churches where it's needed most. We're afraid we will offend someone, or say something racist, or get angry, or make someone mad, or be viewed as belligerent.

I believe many Whites are monocultural simply because they can be. Whites can be educated, live, work, worship, be entertained, and exist in a world that is exclusive to them by virtue of proximity, privilege, media, and opportunity if they so choose. However, Blacks and most every other minority group, are at least bicultural and most likely multicultural because they have little choice. If Blacks or any other subgroup attempt to live, worship, and exist in a world exclusive to them, it is not only virtually impossible but also to their disadvantage since the standards and norms are established by the dominant culture (White, middle-class, Protestant people of northern European descent.) Television and mainstream media alone would prevent the possibility of living in a minority monoculture. Very few of our cities have financial and lending institutions, medical institutions, law enforcement agencies, food services, and city governments that would allow for such a choice.

Basically, our staff did not know what they did not know, which I think is the worst kind of not knowing. For example, to live in squalor is forgivable, but to not be aware of it and have a plan to address it is not. The staff fully comprehended the technical, instructional needs of our children. However, they were not fluent in the non-instructional needs of our students. They did not know the realities, barriers, and struggles of our students and families. They did not know what was funny or offensive to our students and families. They did know what was motivating or frightening to our students and families. My presentation was necessary to educate and expose our staff to a world beyond their own, in hopes they could better understand and ultimately better serve our students. The staff oohed and aahed, laughed and cried, but came away with a deeper understanding and appreciation of our students and families. I think any school that serves children of color and poverty would benefit from witnessing this presentation.

Our staff next read and discussed the book *Black Students, Middle Class Teachers* by Jawanza Kunjufu. He takes an in-depth, poignant look at transcendent and prevailing successes and failures of black children in our urban schools. He addresses hard-hitting facts and statistics that should alarm any caring educator and citizen. Kunjufu provides strategies for the most effective ways to teach and manage students of color. He also offers solutions that will empower schools and parents to overcome the odds.

Over time, the Tulakes staff as a whole shifted from viewing our community with an apathetic lens to viewing it through a lens of understanding, sensitivity, and compassion. Those who rejected the notion of empathy were overwhelmed by those who cared, and they soon chose to either become inextricably woven into our fabric of love or go elsewhere.

We had started the conversation that I now call America's Elephant in the Room—race and privilege/opportunity/access. Many educators are in denial about their own thoughts regarding how they look at people of color and poverty. Some deny that any academic failure is due in part to our attitudes, actions, and failures to relate to our students and the communities in which they live. As a team at Tulakes, we ventured out on this uneasy, uncomfortable voyage for the sake of our students.

Staff Retreat

As I prepared for my second year as principal at Tulakes, nearly half of my first year's staff disembarked our ship. This was due to an increasingly widening chasm between the demographics of our staff and students and the fact that the "new captain on board"—me— was expecting teachers to make internal and external changes. With our new staff team, I needed something consequential to quickly coalesce them. So a few teacher and I planned a fabulous overnight retreat.

The retreat was scheduled approximately thirty miles outside of town in a bucolic area to draw us away from comfort, family, familiarity, and the other distractions of home. We ordered t-shirts to distinguish the new teachers from returning staff— Veterans and Newbies. We played. We ate. We learned about one another. We planned. We did some team building. We ate some more and played more, ending with a familiarity and bonding among all that we could not have anticipated. Eating, playing, talking, and sleeping in close quarters allows things to happen both rapidly and organically like nothing else.

Sadly, in some of our schools, teachers barely even know each other's names, much less anything about their fellow staff as people. Their classrooms may be located at opposite ends of the building or different buildings. Their schedules may never coincide. How can they be a team when they do not even know their teammates?

Conversely, on Tulakes' first day of school, the new teachers were all well-acquainted with each other. They'd already spent time together. The returning teachers were familiar with the incoming staff and also had become closer with one another. In short, we were able to truncate a process that probably would not have otherwise occurred until the middle or end of the school year if it happened at all.

Any team that knows and likes one another is more likely to be successful. As I speak all over the country, I share about my beloved Oklahoma Sooners and the NCAA National Championship team of 2000 that defeated the Florida State Seminoles. The Seminoles had a squad filled with first-round draft picks, but they lost to the Sooners, who were solid underdogs. The Sooners knew one another's strengths. They knew one another's weaknesses. They knew one another's tendencies. They had one another's backs. I would much rather line up my guys as a team against individuals any day.

Since that first staff retreat, this event has become an annual affair. We made every effort to involve everyone, including the custodial and cafeteria staff. The retreat was as customary as open house, faculty meetings, Christmas parties, and everything else we did annually. Our staff retreat set the tone, or better, set us up for success, and galvanized us for the challenging work ahead.

Professional Dress

I imagine this heading is disquieting for some teachers, possibly evoking tremendous angst, but please stay with me. When I arrived at Tulakes, professional dress meant anything that was laundered and "presentable." I am not suggesting that staff dress was disheveled, but it was not as professional as I would have preferred.

I know teachers do not make much money, especially in the state of Oklahoma. I know full well that teachers, particularly in elementary schools, sometimes have to sit on the floor "crisscross applesauce" or go outside and get a little sweaty and dusty, especially in the state of Oklahoma. However, and please do not get perturbed if you are a teacher, our children play sports and perform in the band in all kinds of conditions, sometimes in all-white uniforms. Painters come to our homes to paint in white uniforms. The milkman delivers, or at least used to deliver, milk in a white uniform. The mail is delivered by a person in a uniform. The workers at Walmart, McDonald's, and Kentucky Fried Chicken all wear uniforms. Some of the aforementioned get paid and some do not. Some receive great salaries, and some barely earn a decent wage. They all wear clothing that distinguishes them, that promotes a theme or pride. Why then would teachers do otherwise?

I believe clothes influence behavior. Picture how you walk, talk, or sit when you are dressed in formal clothes as opposed to how you do the same in your most casual wear. I walk, talk, sit, and behave differently when I have on a suit and tie than when I am in a jogging suit. As educators, it matters how we feel about ourselves and how we walk, talk, sit, and act. We need a uniform —professional dress.

Even more important, our clothes influence how others

perceive and respond to us. If children see us as professionals, they are more likely to treat us as such. If parents view us as professionals, they are more likely to treat us as such. In fact, when we don't take care to dress professionally we may be inadvertently communicating a low regard for our roles as educators and those in our charge. As national education leader Renee Moore states:

> Most black parents and students here in the Delta still take great offense at teachers who dress too casually in the classroom, for it sends the nonverbal message that "What I'm doing here really isn't that important," or worse, "the people for whom I'm doing it aren't really that important."[9]

I remember when I first proposed the idea to the staff of eliminating jeans from our wardrobes, at least Monday through Thursday. I did not have authority to outright prohibit jeans, nor did I want to mandate such a change. A majority of the staff embraced and accepted the no-more-jeans idea; a few felt otherwise. I was even contacted by a local newspaper reporter who interrogated me about restricting jeans for my staff. This took me by surprise, but I informed him that my message to the staff had only been a suggestion.

Later, however, the only known dissenter approached me to say that although she did not initially agree with my position, she had since relented. She came to conclude that the good aspects of the wardrobe change outweighed the bad.

Since those early days, our staff became recognized as one of the best-dressed, most professionally attired and performing staffs around. They changed from being a team that perhaps just tolerated the idea of professional apparel to being a staff that embraced being fashionable for the sake of our institution, our profession, our parents, and most of all, our wonderful children.

I understand the potential controversy around this subject. Yet no one will convince me that more professional staff attire did not play a role, at least indirectly, in the turnaround of our school.

Peer Observations

Teachers observing teachers is rare in our public schools, which is astonishing at best. Almost every other profession I am familiar with includes routinely watching, listening to, and learning from others. Surgeons watch other surgeons perform delicate, life-or-death incisions. Lawyers watch other lawyers argue and debate cases that can result in life or death for clients. Preachers watch other preachers orate and exhort their congregants regarding spiritual life and death.

However, when it comes to teaching, where good teaching can breathe life into students and poor teaching can lead to the death of an entire generation of students, educators too often do not observe and seek feedback from their peers. They too often go into their rooms with an "I got it" attitude. It's the children who too often suffer.

Therefore, I asked our teachers to regularly observe one another teach. Although some in their hearts went kicking and scratching since time was a premium for them, they all learned so much from one another. They learned great pedagogical strategies in the various disciplines from one another. They learned great classroom management strategies from one another. They learned great student engagement strategies from one another. They learned great classroom arrangement and setup from one another. What they lost in time, they gained in skill and best practices. Even more, they learned to appreciate, respect, and trust one another even more. I echoed to them over and over that the best professional development was right there on our staff and I fully believed every bit of what I said.

Teacher Hiring Process

Hiring the right people and retaining them is an absolute must for the success of any organization. Thus, one of the best things we did was to hire "highly qualified" staff. But we defined this term differently than the US Congress did in the No Child Left Behind Act of 2001 (changed in 2015 to the Every Student Succeeds Act). They, and therefore the Oklahoma State Department of Education, defined highly qualified early childhood and elementary school teachers as having:

- Option A: Passed a state certification test in level/subject taught, or
- Option B: Completed an undergraduate academic major or coursework equivalent to an undergraduate academic major (24 semester hours of subject-specific coursework) in subject taught as documented by the teacher's official transcript, or
- Option C: Completed a graduate degree in subject taught, or
- Option D: Holds certification through National Board for Professional Teaching Standards in subject taught, or
- Option E: Demonstrated competency in each subject taught based on a High Objective Uniform State Standard of Evaluation (HOUSSE).

Again, there was an entirely different expectation for what it meant to be a highly qualified teacher at our school. Highly qualified had much more to do with your heart than your ability. Our process for hiring teachers first involved contacting references, because we were more interested in the candidate's past and character than we were their GPA or resume. The candidate was not removed from consideration solely on a reference, but we always tried to give more credence to the reputation and mettle of the candidate as witnessed by others who had worked with or known him or her.

Our staff came to believe that it would be better to be moderately understaffed than to have someone with questionable work ethic and character on our staff. It would be better to be deficient in quantity than in quality. In fact, they were more than happy to have too many children in their classes than to have the desired or required teacher-to-student ratio if it meant settling on a subpar teacher to fill the gap.

Consequently, we instituted a rather unique interview process. Approximately seven teachers participated in every interview, not so much to make the hiring selections but rather to share the Tulakes philosophy and culture we had created and which they wholeheartedly were unwilling to compromise.

As principal and as unthreateningly as possible, I asked the same questions of each candidate in order to maintain consistency between the potential teachers. I always smiled, as I was totally aware of the potential intimidation of sitting in a room with eight strangers looking at you. There were the usual questions about experience and teaching philosophy. However, we went much deeper. I asked about their skills and comfort in working with people of poverty and color, and how they would create an environment that would make a child want to avoid getting into trouble, and how far they were willing to go to ensure that every child succeeded. The questions were more about their hearts than their pedagogical skills.

The most important part of the interview was saved for last. After I completed the question portion, the teachers in the room would share the challenges, expectations, and perquisites for working at our school—from their perspective. The teachers would make it clear that working at Tulakes was no walk in the park. They would point out the students' academic and social needs, all of which tested any teacher's perseverance and resilience. They would talk about how our children had suffered too many revolving doors (of adults in and out of their lives) already at such young ages. We were not looking for someone applying for a temporary stay. They would share that we were not seeking teachers who just planned to get to school on time and leave as soon as the bell rang. They wanted new all-in team members, and accountability to that end was not optional.

They all shared—with passion—that our children and families would love their teachers if they were first shown love. They would share with passion that our school was a beacon in the community. They would share with passion how much fun we had as a staff. They would share with passion that all current staff would be helpful and supportive of all new hires. They would share with passion that their own biological children, cousins, nieces, and nephews attended our school (this was huge, and though not a requirement, was the norm). They would share with passion that we were a special and proud staff. They would share with passion that their principal was a fixture, not looking for greener pastures and who loved his staff, students, and their families. They would share with passion that we were called to serve at our school and were looking for people who felt that same calling.

As the interviews evoked great passion from the teachers,

they frequently ended with both the teachers and the candidate in tears. I unequivocally believe that the emotions of the potential hire were due to one of two reasons. Some felt like it had been the interview from hell. They thought, "These Tulakes teachers are crazy as heck if they expect me to pour that much of myself into a job." But more often than not, I think the candidates felt like they had died and gone to teacher heaven. They were praying they would be chosen to join a team of teachers where so many people were bound together by a common thread of love and commitment for children. We had created an incredible staff and knew we had an amazing culture and climate to offer any would-be teacher. They hadn't known such a thing existed.

My intuitions were confirmed when I received phone calls from colleagues who told me they had offered candidates jobs on the spot but were told by them they would not accept an offer until they heard back from Tulakes. Such honesty and candor rarely happens with teacher candidates in general and could not have even been imagined to happen at Tulakes based on how the school was perceived when I first arrived. I give my staff all the credit.

A last-but-not-least critical component to our hiring process was that we were intentional in pursuing people who represented the population of our students and families. We purposefully sought to hire Black and Latino men and women at minimum in proportion to our student body. This was not because I am a black man, but because having a diverse staff brings with it diverse perspectives, and also because our students needed to see role models who looked like them, too. Our children had seen diversity well represented in retail, professional athletics, art, and entertainment. However, in one of the most important professions (one they saw up close on a daily basis), they had seen and experienced far too few teachers of color to give them something to emulate in a place called school.

Respected educator Haim Ginott described well the teacher's heart we were looking for on our staff team:

> I've come to the frightening conclusion that I am the decisive element in the classroom. It's my personal approach that creates the climate. It's my daily mood that makes the weather. As a teacher, I possess a tremendous power to make a child's life miserable or joyous. I can be a tool of torture or an instrument of inspiration. I can humiliate or humor, hurt or heal. In all situations, it is my response that decides whether a crisis will be escalated or de-escalated and a child humanized or dehumanized.[10]

As a result of our unique hiring process, we ended up with a collection of some of the greatest teachers you could find anywhere on earth, from kindergarten to fifth grade, from the office staff to the specials teachers. In addition, our staff turnover rate was extremely low. As a principal, I would have stacked this group of educators against any staff in the country.

Teacher Passion

Finally, it was my expectation that teachers were passionate about the success of their students and willing to do whatever it took for them to succeed. Certainly, like any school, the personalities of our staff ran the gamut of extroversion to introversion. Some filled the room with their presence, while others I had to look for in their classrooms since they were not much bigger than their pupils. However, I asked each teacher to meet with me one-on-one to tell me what passion for student success looked like from his or her point of view. Some got an attaboy, while others were prodded with thoughts on how to grow or augment their passion. I am a firm believer that passion is transferable. I cannot help but wonder what could be achieved if all teachers were passionate about what they did and about student learning. But I can proudly proclaim that every teacher at Tulakes demonstrated such passion. See the Resources page for more on what our passion looked like.

Hire character. Train skill.
—Peter Schutz, executive

DISCUSSION QUESTIONS FOR CHAPTER SIX

1. Have you ever thought about how poverty decades ago differs from poverty today? What are specific examples of the differences?

2. What evidence do you see of the detrimental effects of the increase in drug and alcohol abuse, incarceration, and poverty?

3. What are your thoughts on the concept of being "monocultural"?

4. Do you feel teacher dress has any effect on student perception, interaction, and success? How so?

5. Would you choose to use the process of peer observations? Why or why not?

6. What are your thoughts on the hiring process implemented at Tulakes? What do you like and what do you dislike about their process?

7. What role do you think passion has in effective teaching?

7

CHARTING A NEW COURSE

We can, whenever and wherever we choose, successfully teach
all children whose schooling is of interest to us.
We already know more than we need to do that.
Whether or not we do it finally depends on
how we feel about the fact that we haven't so far.
—Ronald Edmonds, educator and author

At Tulakes we diligently implemented game-changing practices that enabled our school to make a 180-degree turn and ultimately become a great school. It just made sense to me and to us that if one method was not working, then we needed to try another. It has been said that "necessity is the mother of invention," so it is incumbent on all of us as educators to approach our methods, procedures, and practices differently.

Student Behavior

Student behavior or misbehavior is one of the most consistently and conspicuously troublesome issues in schools all over America. Countless experts and researchers have written books about this topic alone. But discipline often gets more attention than it deserves as school districts spend hours talking about it in staff training; as school districts spend hours in teacher negotiations; as school districts spend hours in student hearings; as schools spend hours of the day with students and parents instead of instruction and learning. Yes, some of the cost and time is justifiable, but as much as we know about the topic, we should be much further along the "effective management continuum" than we are.

Student misconduct or failure to adhere to all our rules and demands is not some new phenomenon! Smile if you remember watching *To Sir, With Love*; *Welcome Back, Kotter*; *Happy Days*; *Saved by the Bell*; or *Dangerous Minds*. Mischief and minors always have and always will coexist. Even the Apostle Paul acknowledged this when he said, "When I was a child, I talked like a child, I thought like a child, I reasoned like a child. When I became a man, I put the ways of childhood behind me."[11]

Kids have always tested the limits, made poor choices, and been prone to succumb to negative peer pressure. They are kids. I know I used to be one, and I hope you remember you were as well. I tried to hammer this fact home to our staff. With a little prodding, they remembered they had once been kids, too.

I was *not* asking teachers to tolerate or dismiss inappropriate behavior. Remember, I am from the old school. Back in my day, you got "it" at school, and you got "it" again when you got home. You got "it" from almost anybody, especially if your parents knew them or they were someone of good repute. Respect and compliance was not negotiable then, and neither is it now with me.

However, some things have changed drastically since then, and I believe we need to make some adjustments accordingly. For the first time in modern history, some of our children actually may not know right from wrong. Fewer and fewer of them are being raised by parents or guardians who stress the Golden Rule of "do unto others, as you would have them to do unto you." Fewer and fewer of them are being raised by the village of mamas and daddies, grandmas and grandpas, aunts and uncles, church-going neighbors, mom and pop proprietors, Lions, Rotary, and Kiwanis club members, and more who raised some of us.

Instead, some children today have no positive support network in their lives. One story to illustrate this occurred when I first became an assistant principal more than twenty-five years ago. The school bell had rung, and the halls were empty with the exception of one young man. I told him to have a good day, and I would see him tomorrow. About fifteen minutes passed, and I saw him again, still lingering in the halls. I told him to head home, as it was time for the custodial staff to secure the building. Low and behold, about twenty minutes later, with my things in hand and heading for the exit door, I saw him again and asked why he was still in the building. He looked me square in my face and said, "Mr. Roland, if I go home with nothing in my hand, I am going to get my @*% beat."

That young man was being taught to do things that I and almost everyone else in my day was taught not to do. What scares me the most is the fact that this event occurred years before the children in our schools were even born, and that society has declined even more since then. Moreover, I am concerned that this young man probably represents more households than any of us would like to believe or imagine. It does not make it OK, but many of our students' parents are incarcerated. It does not make it OK, but many of our students' parents are struggling to just get by. It does not make it OK, but many of our students are raising themselves. It does not make it OK, but the influence of video games, music, and television has not been altogether positive.

Just look at some of the lyrics from well-known hip-hop artists Snoop Dogg and Wiz Khalifa in "Young, Wild & Free."[12]

So what we get drunk?
So what we smoke weed?
We're just having fun
We don't care who sees
So what we go out?
That's how it's supposed to be
Living young and wild and free

Therefore, in light of all of the above influences on our children, we as educators must take an entirely different approach in responding to behavior today. We must be proactive, as opposed to reactive.

I pressed my staff to consider the possibility that at least 50 percent of the discipline problems educators encounter are caused by their own action or inaction. Think about it. You've heard it said that "a failure to plan is a plan to fail." Why would that be any different in a classroom? Why would we position two children who we know do not get along to sit in proximity to one another? Why would we not follow our discipline plan? Why would we not try to make our instruction so engaging, rewarding, and fun that to not be allowed to participate is punishment in itself? Why would we not reflect daily and make adjustments? Why would we not seek out and observe others who have a propensity for maintaining an environment that is more conducive to learning? Why would we ever be less than attentive or leave students unattended? Why would we not seek to have win-win situations rather than win-lose situations with our kids? The onus is on us as the adults to leave very little room for ambiguity and lack of follow-through.

As a side note, I have shared with educators for as long as I can remember that as human beings it is difficult for some and impossible for others to forgive when they have been wrongfully punished. Think how you would react if given a speeding ticket when you were going five miles an hour below the speed limit? Therefore, we should err on the side of caution before ever punishing a child without absolute proof.

For example, a master teacher who was extremely loving, fair, and kind brought a student to my office once for stealing. He had been the only student in the room so he must have taken the item, right? The student vehemently denied it at first, but after a little interrogation, admitted to the misdeed. However, within minutes, a little girl came to the office to confess she had actually been the culprit. When I called the young man back in and asked why he took responsibility for something he did not do, he told me he would rather confess to his teacher who told him she would still love and forgive him rather than having her think ill of him and possibly hold it against him. Again, we should err on the side of caution before punishing a child without absolute proof.

In one last-minute idea and in hope of inspiring teachers just before a faculty meeting, I asked a staff member to randomly video a handful of students to tell what they wished their teachers knew about them. I'll never forget one rambunctious fourth grader, who faced formidable odds at home, who said, "I wish my teacher knew that I am a good person and that it is hard for me to sit still for long periods of time." No teacher looked at a wiggly young lad the same after hearing that!

I also asked—if not insisted—that my staff teach appropriate behavior in the same manner they taught any other discipline. I asked them to teach the rules and expectations just like we teach the ABCs, 2 + 2, subject-verb agreement, and the Constitution. We would not yell or become angry if the students failed to grasp the concepts easily. Instead, we would patiently teach and reteach, perhaps differently until the student mastered the practice. We might teach them before school, after school, during lunch or recess, but we would teach them nonetheless. It worked.

Another novel concept was the idea of asking teachers to rethink the way we approach corrective action for students. I asked them to focus their attention on the cessation of the behavior rather than punitive actions.

Sure, some offenses require consequences and administrative action, but many times they do not. For example if there is a skirmish on the playground, could we not counsel students, allow them to apologize, notify a parent, and consider the matter closed? If a student uses inappropriate language, especially when angry or anxious, could we not explain that the language is just not appropriate at school, get the talk to cease, notify a parent, and consider the matter closed?

I'm showing my age here, but what did Desi Arnaz do on the *I Love Lucy Show* when he got angry? He spoke in his native tongue. That is the same default reaction of many of our students under similar conditions; they mimic what they hear at home and consider it normal. In essence, if a student breaks rules that are not severe violations, is it always necessary to write a referral and send the student to the office? At Tulakes, we wanted to eliminate most situations from ever getting that far, and it worked.

Finally, I urged my teachers to respond to inappropriate behavior and administer consequences, when necessary, just like a good police officer would. The officer who pulls over a motorist ideally first inquires whether the driver is aware of the violation. If the driver is not, the officer politely explains, with the hopes that the mistake will be corrected and not repeated in the future. The officer may ask additional questions. Is there an emergency? Do your turn signals and lights operate properly? Are you OK medically? In the end, if a ticket is warranted, it is assessed professionally and with composure. The officer does not yell or become angry. He may even at the end say, "Have a nice day." It worked.

We also wanted to be sure that our manner of addressing behavior was consistent throughout the school. A rule violation was treated the same in Mrs. Brown's class as it was in Mrs. White's class. As a staff, we came up with the following:

School-Wide Assertive Discipline Plan

Teachers are required (if possible) to notify parents of students with behavior problems before referring those students to the office except in cases of severe behavior or emergency. If problem behavior continues after the teacher has followed the plan and exhausted all methods:

- Step 1: Warning (warm and kind)
- Step 2: First consequence (example: miss five minutes of recess)
- Step 3: Second and third consequences (example: miss ten minutes of recess, then miss ALL of recess)
- Step 4: The counselor will visit with the child and sit in the classroom with the child to get him or her back to participating. Have the appropriate form filled out and ready to give the student when he or she comes back into the room. While the counselor is in the room, the parent needs to be called by the teacher or counselor.

- Step 5: If the behavior continues, the child receives a fifth check and a referral to the office. Administration will decide on the consequence (time-out in office, suspension, etc).
- Step 6: Typically, after a second referral (within a reasonable amount of time), the child will go home with a letter stating that the child cannot return to school until the parent visits with the counselor or an administrator.

High Expectations

This section on high expectations goes hand-in-hand with the section on discipline. As a principal, I expected our students to thrive both in and out of the classroom, academically as well as behaviorally.

I knew my high expectations were an uphill battle for our children. Many of our students endured and confronted formidable odds economically, educationally, and socially. How were they supposed to successfully navigate two worlds (school and the rest of their lives) that were often polar opposites?

They teetered in one world outside of school, where education was at the bottom of the list of priorities due to circumstances beyond their control. They then tottered in another world at school, where acquiring knowledge was at the top of the list of priorities. They lived in one world where high volume was the social norm and another where quietness was expected and demanded, one where physicality and force were required for survival and another where mental adeptness was prized. They lived in one world where some adults taught and demanded of them to do one thing and went to school in another world where adults taught and demanded of them to do another.

Nevertheless, I did my best to insist and instill character in our children. They were never allowed to say "huh, what, un-un, naw, or yeah" to me or any adult, including their parent in my presence. Instead, they were expected to say "pardon or excuse me; yes or yes, sir; no or no, ma'am." That is the way I addressed them as well. I tried to model what I expected from them. I asked teachers and parents to hold students to the same standards.

I might add that we had outside help in this endeavor. We had partner organizations that helped train our children—Life-Church, Novo Bible Club, Whiz Kids, In the Gap, and Cherokee Hills Baptist Church. I was picky about the groups I gave access to our kids. I wanted them to be positive, committed role models for them. The groups that came impacted our children in positive ways that are hard to quantify.

The staff and I told the students every chance we had that we believed in them and expected them to achieve academically and conduct themselves appropriately. We needed to convince them to believe and expect as much for themselves.

Let me pause here and explain something about high expectations, especially as it relates to conduct. First, I find it unacceptable to hold students to higher expectations than we as adults hold for ourselves. I have little to no tolerance for the teacher who says, "We have to teach them to be responsible" when I have witnessed that same teacher demonstrate irresponsibility. I think that's what they call the pot calling the kettle black. Second, I think the expression "high expectations" should never equate to "no mistakes tolerated." No one can be perfect. We all make mistakes. But we can rise to higher and higher expectations.

I stressed high expectations. Beliefs can be transformative if they're shared and acted upon. We upheld these expectations as a staff, and the children started to believe, too. Belief became contagious.

First thing every morning after announcements we recited our school creed, and our teachers became masters of instilling self-affirmations. It was music to my ears to hear our children reciting the creed in unison, from our four-year-olds all the way up to our fifth graders. They were learning to believe in themselves.

Excellent Instruction

To be the school we wanted to be, we had to have excellent teaching. Teachers were expected to make use of every teachable moment because we had no time to waste at our school. We knew full well the research on the vocabulary deficits of children of poverty entering school versus those of middle class and beyond. Christopher Bergland writes:

> By age three, it is believed that children growing up in poor neighborhoods or from lower-income families may hear up to 30 million fewer words than their more privileged counterparts.[13]

We knew that evenings and weekends were not necessarily spent in quiet solitude with a bright light over the kitchen table doing homework, learning multiplication facts, practicing spelling words, or listening to a book being read aloud. Thus, even in those morning announcements, read by students, we asked the teachers to teach well.

So our students heard:

> Students, you know what day it is! Yes, it's Marrrrrrvelous Monday! We're so glad you're here today because it's important to be at school EVERY DAY, focused, on time, and

in your uniform. That's what helps us achieve and sets us apart from other schools. Teachers, teach us well from bell to bell, and we'll do our best to pass our daily test. That's a winning combination and will certainly make it a Marvelous Monday here at Tulakes.

This was largely an unnecessary reminder since our teachers began instruction before the bell rang. The teachers took it upon themselves to begin instruction when the kids entered their classes, which they encouraged them to do as early as possible. Most teachers took advantage of *every* teachable moment. Most took bathroom breaks as a class to avoid students going out of the class one-at-a-time and missing instruction, so it was routine for children to have books in hand while standing or sitting in the halls and going to and from lunch. If the students were not reading or practicing some skill independently, they were receiving direct instruction from the teachers. Always teaching!

Effective instruction was a school-wide priority. Classroom walkthroughs occurred daily, with feedback provided privately as needed or during staff meetings when it seemed best. I would share what great things I had observed or what practices I thought we needed to change.

We expected every student to be engaged. I asked teachers to stop the practice of hand-raising to answer questions. If permitted, some students would answer most or all of the questions, while others would answer few or none. You do not have to be an experienced teacher to know that this is not a good practice. Some teachers thus used popsicle sticks to increase randomness, while others were just adept at making sure to prompt every student.

Another crucial requirement was the basic elements of every lesson. We emphasized that, regardless of evaluation models, the students needed to know what they were being taught and what they were expected to learn. A football, basketball, or baseball coach would not just toss his team a ball and tell them to practice. He or she would provide a goal or objective for any given drill or practice. The coach then would show the team how to execute the drill and observe them performing the skill until it had been mastered. The same was expected in our Tulakes' classrooms. We required the objective and goal for all lesson plans written on the board to ensure that the children knew what was expected. This was then followed with expert teaching, independent practice, and feedback.

Our teachers were asked to watch and reflect on what good coaches do. Coaches stress winning. Coaches emphasize giving your best. Coaches demonstrate passion. Coaches explain. Coaches model. Coaches challenge. Coaches have do-overs. Coaches adjust. Coaches allow others to demonstrate. Coaches praise, praise, and PRAISE some more!

In the end, we adopted the idea that if students did not learn, then we had not taught well. Overall, effective instruction translated into learning. The onus was on us.

Professional Learning Communities

Professional Learning Communities have become popular in schools all over the country. If you're an educator, you're familiar with them. PLCs are meant to foster collaborative learning among teachers and provide a way for them to work together toward practice-based professional learning. The data is clear that if teachers plan together as a team for the success of children, the likelihood of failure diminishes substantially.

However, this only works when the teachers do not treat this as just another perfunctory meeting they have to attend. They must focus the meeting on data, student work, instruction, best practices, fixing what is broken, and celebrating what is going well.

The concept of required PLC meetings, once a week during teacher plan time, was initially met with great resistance in many schools across our nation. Tulakes, however, was ahead of the curve since a similar construct had already been introduced to us from a professional development company a year prior to our district's adoption of the concept.

Our staff was ready to dedicate the time and effort for real learning communities. This was because our staff willingly embraced any concept that worked to benefit our students. Our Tulakes fourth grade team had the highest reading scores in the district. The credit went to the PLCs and their teachers. It was such a joy to see their professional discussions, like engineers or military strategists. They got into the how, why, and what of their work. They hashed it out. I will never forget when one of the PLC team leaders said, "We do not have time to be embarrassed about our weaknesses or failures or to brag about our strengths or successes. We lay it all out to help and be helped by one another. These are all of our kids."

We asked the best and most productive teams to share their best practices at staff meetings so they could lead the rest of us in what we could do better. They agreed, and we all benefited. Most of our best professional development was free and already within the walls of our school.

Core Values

It eventually dawned on me and our team that it would be beneficial to evaluate and cultivate our school's ethos. We knew how we went about our business and took great pride in it, but what could we say defined us?

"Ethos" is a Greek word meaning character, is used to describe the guiding beliefs or ideals that characterize a community, nation, or ideology. One of the major undertakings of our staff advisory team was to help create our school's core values or ethos. The values would later require the entire staff's buy in, but we needed a place to start.

I had my own ideas for our core values, lofty and ambitious ones. The team knew this. However, the values ultimately had to be a "we thing." I would throw out bait every chance I got from individual conversations with teachers to formal meetings. When time came to put something down on paper, there was little need for me to chime in. Again, there is nothing sweeter than hearing your leadership team promulgating the same lofty and ambitious goals as you! As I even think about it again, I am beaming from ear to ear.

Here are the core values we agreed on and promoted at Tulakes:

#1 *We never let a child fail!*

Example: Mrs. Kenyelle "High Expectations" Waiters required her children to chant or recite whenever transitioning from class to class. It was a special treat to see them chanting in perfect unison and perfect cadence, "We are Tulakes Twisters and a class of excellence, here to achieve and be the best we can be." Chanting was one thing, but what happened in the class was the proof.

She intentionally instilled a growth-mindset in the students. The focus was not nearly as much about mastery as it was on improving. They celebrated any and all progress. With skill-based, small group instruction, every student made sizable progress. The students could visibly see where they started, and they pushed to do just a little better. Almost all achieved mastery. I would liken it to a personal trainer.

Ultimately, she did not hold the students at fault for any lack of success. She saw any failure as her failure, and she did not like losing. In fact, her students were allowed to give her a daily grade for her instruction. I loved it! It was just part of the culture.

#2 *We do whatever it takes!*

Example: Mrs. Maggie "Extreme" Oaks, who had just recently married, walked in my office one day to get my thoughts on a matter. One of her student's moms, of another color I might add and who was about to have a baby any day, informed Mrs. Oaks she had no one to watch her other small children while she was in the hospital. Mrs. Oaks was considering watching the children herself and asked me as her boss if I approved. I told her she must be out of her mind, but I also looked her in the face and told her that when you care about people, you do crazy stuff and that was just who we are. If she was comfortable, then so was I. She watched the mom's children until she was released from the hospital. I loved it. It was just part of the culture.

Example: Mrs. Kathy "Extreme" Whitinger walked into my office and informed me that one of her more "high maintenance" children had just moved away. She proceeded to matter-of-factly inform me that she would be more than happy to take such a child from another teacher if needed. This is almost unheard of in school business. She ended up taking a little boy who was a handful (super high maintenance) from a lower grade. She individualized his lessons, and he ended up staying with her for three years, improving in his behavior in the process. I loved it! It was just part of the culture.

Example: Mrs. Melissa "Extreme" Meek had the single parent of one her students suddenly become hospitalized with a near-death illness. The prognosis was grim for some time. The child and her older siblings had no relatives in the state to care for them. Mrs. Meek and her family took the children in, feeding, caring, and loving on them until the parent was dismissed from the hospital. I loved it. It was just part of the culture.

#3 *We accept and embrace diversity!*

Example: Mr. Jason "Diversity" Clark was from a part of the state with little to no residents of color. He joined our staff with perhaps something to prove to us as well as himself. He quickly proved and even exceeded his value. He demonstrated his excellence to the kids by volunteering to teach an all-boys class, which he did with great creativity and wit, building fabulous relationships and helping every one of them make measurable academic gains.

He did not stop there. He started after-school programs like earth, chess, and debate clubs. The mutual respect and admiration between him and his students was wonderful to behold. I loved it! It was just part of the culture.

Even more impressive, this same gentleman became our school's gifted teacher. I will not wax long on this topic, but a remarkable thing, a miracle of sorts occurred shortly after he transitioned to this position. In our school of poverty and color, the number of children qualifying for gifted service tripled, almost overnight as he was aggressive in searching out and identifying our children. I loved it! It was just part of the culture.

#4 We teach beyond the curriculum!

Example: Mr. Brett "Extracurricular" Payne was masterful in engaging children in and out of class. He worked hard during school to ensure his students' achievement in the classroom, resulting in some of the highest test scores in the district. They loved him, and he loved them more.

Much of the outside connection happened after school via sports. He and his grade-level teammates started off by having our children participate in a YMCA league basketball program on weekends. I cannot tell you how many evenings and weekends they sacrificed to transport, feed, and coach these boys and girls. I had never seen that level of selflessness in my entire career. When some surrounding schools heard of our success and pure unadulterated fun, they joined in too. This eventually led to a district-wide elementary soccer and basketball program.

What started out with our fifth grade teachers engaging with their students after school eventually became an expectation that every grade would do something extra with their students in one fashion or another. Some connected with students through sports, some through clubs, some through dancing, some through cheerleading, and some through other means. I loved it! It just became part of the culture.

The payoff for all of this was huge and unanticipated. First of all, we were able to use participation as an incentive to encourage making good choices and working hard. Students who were once marginally interested in school all of a sudden were very motivated. We had a more-captive audience in the classroom and improved character development at the same time.

Second, some of our most hard-to-reach parents became more accessible. We took advantage of encountering these parents in another setting, outside of school, where their guards were down, and they were more appreciative of our sacrifice of our personal time. It did not hurt either that we were cheering on their kiddos. I loved it! It was just part of the culture.

#5 *We support and hold one another accountable!*

Example: Mrs. Debra "No-Nonsense" Clark was one of my teachers who never rotated off the advisory team. She was small in stature and relatively soft-spoken. She taught our youngest students, so she was the first to introduce them to the world of academia. I always thought her formal mannerisms and elegant comportment seemed better suited for a high school or a college Consumer Science class.

Mrs. Clark soon became famous (or infamous) for two utterances, which were always timely in meetings. The first statement pertained to kids. Having been a stable fixture in our school for seven or eight years, she knew that many of the upper-grade children had sat in her lap and been tenderly nourished academically as well as emotionally. She would teasingly say (kind of) to other teachers, "You mess with my kids, and I will grab a bat and chase you down." Albeit tiny and petite, she was a fierce mama bear. She loved those kids!

The other declaration communicated her own selfless commitment to her children and the rest of the staff. She would say to the other teachers, "When it's time for me to go, I expect you, my colleagues to tell me." In other words, she never wanted it to be said that she was one of those teachers that stayed too long and was basically a useless and ineffective fixture. She wanted to make a difference until she was no longer a difference maker and wanted to be told by her colleagues if she didn't recognize it first.

Both of these proclamations went down in Tulakes' lore. They were oft-repeated. They sent a message and spread a theme of accountability that became woven into the fabric and ethos of our school. I loved it! It was just part of the culture of our school.

With regard to all the above, there is so much more to tell! To mention how grade-level teams picked up students on spring and summer breaks to tutor would take too long. To mention how grade-level teams had picnics for families with donations or funds from their own pockets would take too long. To mention how grade-level teams rewarded students for passing tests and good behavior with exhausting sleepovers at the school would take too long. To tell you all the amazing individual acts of dedication and love would take much too long. Just know that I loved it and it was just part of our culture.

I cannot and will not take the credit for what these amazing people accomplished, but I might take a fragment of the credit for creating the fertile soil in which their splendor could bloom.

Why Teachers Matter

But perhaps one of our students, Nautica Thomas, said best how amazing our Tulakes' staff were and how much they mattered. She said:

> I'll tell you why teachers matter. Just to walk in a school and feel wanted is every student's dream. To be honored for even the smallest things to the most major is encouraging—to be given the wings of every teacher that walks Tulakes' halls is amazing.
>
> And who knew I'd be loved just because of who I am?
>
> Before I experienced Tulakes, all I knew was that the community I called home was full of despair and crime infested. Crime: meaning hearing gunshots, screaming and arguing almost ceaselessly around the clock. Crime: meaning

too afraid to lay down my head and dream of something beautiful because the darkness of this world appeared to be trying to deliberately destroy kids like me. Crime: meaning such a horrifying place we couldn't look out the window without hurting. That was the way I viewed life.

I believe no child should go through life like that. I was on a path to drifting into the ways of the projects because it was hard to identify who I really was until I walked into Tulakes with a collared navy shirt and khaki pants, greeted by a collection of some of the most amazing educators on God's green earth. I walked those halls with such curiosity, because this school walked as a big family.

Let me tell you a little about that family of teachers. They did things for students that are not in any teacher's job description. For example, one of my teacher's slogans for her class was: "Class of excellence!" Those words influenced the way I walked, the way I talked, the way I behaved and the way I thought. I knew that I was expected to walk with my head up, look forward and speak with intelligence and respect. I was expected to handle things with dignity. I had to because most of the time she was watching my every move. She expected so much and told us so every day.

Another example is that no one said that to become a teacher you must feed children, take them to and from school, and buy them uniforms and supplies with your own hard-earned money. But because my teachers said there wasn't anything they wouldn't do for us, they sacrificed their time to make sure that some of us were taken to and from school. Oh, they were quite a family!

And, like any family there should be a man of the house and it was clear to see that man was my principal, Mr. Lee Roland.

Mr. Roland is a unique man. He does what many fathers don't, including just being around. Mr. Roland goes above and beyond because he wants everyone to succeed in life. He is an encouraging, hardworking, selfless, beautiful, God-fearing, helpful, wonderful, humanitarian, optimistic, funny, flexible, and detailed man. Yes, he is a very detailed man. Even if it takes him ten hours to get to a point, we still love him.

During every assembly, Mr. Roland ALWAYS finds a way to squeeze in a sermon, sometimes brief and sometimes not, but always touching hearts with his words. Hearing and watching him inspired me to become even better to let people know that you could come from the most hopeless place in America, yet end at the most honored place on earth, the White House.

At the end of the day, Mr. Roland's words added up to us striving harder and reaching for a dream.

So you ask why do teachers matter? I realized that's what my family of teachers and administrators lived for.... which is us students! With their guidance, I became a track star, speaker, actress, singer, dancer, stomper and an all around super star, and a 2013 Black History Thunder Essay Hero Winner.

Ladies and Gentlemen: in closing, I matter! That's why teachers matter.

In determining the right people, the good-to-great companies placed greater weight on character attributes than on specific educational background, practical skills, specialized knowledge, or work experience.
—Jim Collins, author and management consultant

DISCUSSION QUESTIONS FOR CHAPTER SEVEN

1. What value do you see in having high expectations for children, especially those from backgrounds with more challenges?
2. What are your thoughts of utilizing community resources to help promote character and learning in the school? Is it time well spent or not?
3. Do you agree with the statement: "If students did not learn, we did not teach"?
4. Have you ever heard of Professional Learning Communities? Would you be interested in participating in something like that?
5. What are your thoughts on Tulakes Elementary Core Values? Describe how you agree or disagree with any of them.
6. Would your students say that teachers matter? Do they feel that school is a place of refuge and love? If not, what are you willing to do to change how they feel?

8

A STELLAR CREW

*Outstanding leaders go out of their way to boost
the self-esteem of their personnel. If people believe
in themselves, it's amazing what they can accomplish.*
—Sam Walton, businessman and philanthropist

Staff Advisory

I was not terribly interested in our district's policies and procedures, the negotiated agreement with the teacher's union, or the
stated function of the "staff advisory" process for the district. I
didn't set out to purposely violate any statutes or policy, but I
wanted to have a team to help me steer our ship in the right direc-
tion and get us to our desired destination as quickly and effi-
ciently as possible. I wanted some junior captains.

Our staff was quickly becoming known for going the extra
mile, but these advisory team teachers excelled even more. Their
meetings with me were sometimes long and arduous. I asked
them to dream with me and look at things differently to envision

our school as the best, our children as the best, our parents as the best, and ourselves as the best. They allowed me to push them beyond their comfort zones and share my passion.

Thankfully, the advisory position did come with a small stipend, which helped at least a little since teacher pay in Oklahoma has consistently been among the lowest in the nation. However, I have little doubt that almost every teacher who served on the committee would have done so without remuneration. They were honored to lead and even more honored to serve. They had the dedication I was looking for in captains.

I selected a teacher from every grade each year to serve as a leader for his or her respective team. They were not asked to be "yes men or women," but were expected to be leaders for our cause, which was to "leave no child behind." They also were expected to work collaboratively toward our goal. I was well aware that sometimes having certain personalities would or could result in me making more concessions or harder for us to reach consensus, but my goal was success not simplicity.

The primary criteria for this role included being someone who would lead by example. Our school was replete with teachers who would arrive early, stay late, practice professionalism, go beyond beyond, love all children, love all children, and love ALL children! Therefore, I had a plethora of candidates to select from in every grade every year. It was a good problem to have.

Another key component was that they would more or less agree to be appendages of me and the rest of the advisory team. As the principal, I was inevitably going to sometimes make unpopular decisions and announcements. Perhaps something like: "Effective immediately, all staff are expected to supervise students at recess in strategic positions rather than stand in clusters that do not allow for all children to be supervised." Hopefully everyone would be on board with such a manifesto, but if not…. On other occasions, it could be a matter of consensus. Perhaps something like: Let's all agree to wear black and white for parent orientation with a ten to two vote in favor. The team leader was expected to communicate to their team that, "This is now the expectation," or "This is what WE decided." It was the expectation that they would not return to their team with negativity saying that "This is something Mr. Roland is harping on," or "This is something that everyone else but me decided." Unless they could persuade me and others to take a different course of action, they were expected to be all for one and for all.

As a principal, it was music to my ears when I attended grade-level meetings and heard my teacher leaders challenging their fellow teammates on matters of instruction, dress, professionalism, character, work ethic, dedication, and more. Their messages carried significant weight because it was coming from one of them, a colleague as opposed to the boss. Thus, if their team leader supported the idea, it must be doable and reasonable. Again, it was all I could do not to jump on top of a desk and break out into the Cupid Shuffle when I would sit in these meetings and witness the championing of high expectations.

I couldn't know how the messages were conveyed when I was not able to attend, but I trust that more often than not, they were shared as expected. The staff advisory team undoubtedly played a huge and invaluable role in our ascension to greatness as a school.

Teacher of the Year

In Oklahoma, each year every school selects a Teacher of the Year. This is someone who embodies all the qualities of excellence we expect to see in a teacher, one who talks the talk and walks the walk. Those fortunate enough to be chosen as T.O.Y. at their individual schools can then be in the running for their respective district T.O.Y. District winners then become candidates for the the State T.O.Y.

As the principal, I never played a direct role in our T.O.Y. election process. I wanted to avoid any bias or favoritism. However, I implored the staff to watch out for basing their choice merely on longevity, popularity, sympathy, or anything other than teacher excellence. I wanted to keep the bar high and thus preserve it as a truly meaningful bestowal. I wanted the teachers to select a person they would want to teach their own children. This ultimately became a very difficult chore for our staff since our faculty was brimming with individuals who fit that bill—a principal's dream!

A T.O.Y. celebration is usually marked with a little party, a gift for the winner like a golden apple or a plaque, and perhaps a few tepid remarks of recognition. But the T.O.Y. celebrations at Tulakes were truly special and played a significant role in our school turnaround.

One year I asked our Teacher of the Year winner to allow us to video her in action, executing the most important part of her job. I wanted to record her teaching while her students were engaged and learning....

She agreed, and this served both as celebration, but also a sort of sneaky site-level professional development. As the teachers watched the video, they were asked to take note of any and every best practice and to share their observations with one another. I could not have anticipated a better outcome. The teachers learned from a real practitioner and one of their very own.

To push the envelope just a bit farther, we decided we would add videos of student and peer testimonials on behalf of the T.O.Y. Last, but not least, I asked the T.O.Y. to write a one-page philosophical statement on how he or she approached the job. I wanted to totally illumine the teacher as well as a heartfelt appeal to fellow colleagues, with the hope that anyone in need of a little invigoration and motivation would walk away inspired. Our T.O.Y. became a significant, new tradition for a culture of excellence.

Our T.O.Y. celebrations established and conveyed the message that mediocrity was not welcome at our school. And personally, my view is that there should be more Teachers of the Year chosen from schools with harder-to-teach students. Many teachers can have success with students from stable, middle-income homes. However, it takes a truly excellent teacher to bring success to students from unstable, lower-income situations.

But our teachers truly were amazing. See for yourselves their passion and commitment in their speeches.

Kenyelle Waiters, fourth-grade teacher, 2012–2013

I don't just teach with passion. I teach with a craving for my students to learn. My objective is that my excitement will translate and reflect in my children, and they too will be caught up in the content. I teach with compassion to ensure that I won't ever give up on a child, nor will I allow a child to give up on himself or herself. I teach with concern and continuous reflection to keep myself in check. I teach with care and cultivation to safeguard the growing minds and hearts of my children. I teach with candor because this is a real world we live in, and I feel an obligation to tell our kids and their family members like it T-I-S (as we say in my class)! I teach with catchy phrases and catchy tunes that might annoy some teachers and students, but the important lyrics are burned to my kids' hard drive and will be brought to their remembrance in years to come.

I teach with chairs. Now I know this sounds weird, so let me explain... I am a little vertically challenged, as my big brothers Mr. Payne and Mr. Jeffries so eloquently put it. So I use chairs in my classroom to "get tall" every now and then. Many of you have walked in and caught me standing on my blue chairs instructing as if I were instructing at ground level. My students LOVE when Mrs. Waiters "gets tall"! My theatrics cause all eyes and ears to be on me, and my students are entertainingly engaged in the lesson.

I teach like a champion as I face the daily trials and tribulations this profession brings. Now, teaching like a champion doesn't mean I'm the best. It means I'm a fighter. I'm determined. I persevere. I don't just want to survive, I want to conquer my challenges. The champion in me is a model for how I want my students and their families to face life.

I teach despite circumstances, mine and my children's. In spite of a rough morning with my husband, my daughter, or the traffic, I check my attitude in the car. Checking my attitude at the door is too late for me. Every morning I have a group of kids standing at the door to greet me before I even get out of my car. They rush me and my daughter with their hugs, smiles, and helpful hands. Former students, current students, students that are just getting to know me, and students I've never met before. It doesn't matter how cold it is, or what door I come in, somebody is always embracing me, and I hear shouts of "Good Morning, Mrs. Waiters!"

Many days I've wondered, "Lord, what have I done to be seen as so worthy in their eyes? I don't deserve this love and admiration." Then God reminds me it's not about me. It's all for *his* glory. I'm merely God's earthly vessel for his light to shine through me.

Children in my class learn early on that Mrs. Waiters' expectations don't change according to their circumstances. They know and understand that educational business has to be taken care of, and we cannot let excuses keep us from doing just that. However, my students know that I am empathetic, and that I can equip them with the tools to manipulate their circumstances into building blocks of triumph. My relationships, which are a vital piece of our work, are meaningful and have been built up so that my children know they can come to me, call, or text me concerning anything that is troubling them: homework, family, friends, or just to talk and enjoy conversation. They appreciate me getting to know their older and younger siblings. They love that I know their favorite foods and shows. I celebrate their personal strengths and help them improve their weaknesses. Because of this, they honor my request of not using their circumstances as an excuse not to become excellent.

I teach with competence. We have all been made capable of educating children. We're difference-makers. If you have the ability to do good things, then you have the responsibility to do good things. Here at Tulakes, we have the ability to do GREAT things because of our unique makeup. Therefore, I believe we have the responsibility to do GREAT things.

I teach with closure. Each academic lesson eventually comes to an end. This is when, hopefully, all the puzzle pieces come together, and the children have a grand understanding of the relevance of the lesson and how it can be applied to their lives. During this closure I want to attempt to make all that I just shared with them relevant and hope that I've given them something they can apply to their lives or careers.

Lindsey Cofer, fourth-grade teacher, 2013–2014

In my time as an educator, I have realized that my worth and effectiveness goes far beyond a single test score. I am not just teaching my students to master the skills on the fourth grade PASS objectives, but I instill a champion mindset into my students. Of course their test scores are important, but I also push them to their limit and set the highest of expectations. I want them to see they are overcomers. I am determined to produce a class of difference-makers.

Each year I am greeted with a different group of twenty-three to twenty-five students, all with a story yet to be told. It is my job to unravel their stories. Making a connection and building a relationship with my students and their families is one of the most important aspects of my job. If I am able to capture a child's heart, I have her mind and focus as well.

Many teachers are able to build only surface-level relationships by doing the bare minimum of what needs to be done during school hours. An outstanding teacher is one who goes beyond the surface. My personal philosophy is to do whatever it takes. I have attended birthday parties, Little League games, recitals, first communions, and countless other events that were important in the lives of my students, to show them I am more than just "Mrs. Cofer, their fourth grade teacher."

I hope to convey that I care about each student as a whole person, not only what happens in my classroom. I am available for contact at all times, whatever the issue may be. I constantly tell my students that I will not allow them to leave my classroom thinking they are a failure. Failing is not their destiny.

I enjoy showing them popular current figures who have overcome obstacles in their lives. I share personal stories of my own adversity to instill a hopeful mindset. I help my students understand they can and will achieve excellence by giving them opportunities to set goals throughout the year and aiding them as they track their progress toward the goal.

I reassure parents I am not only here to teach their children, but support them. These relationships become extremely rewarding when I see the love and care I pour into my students being reciprocated. The hugs in the hallway, the smiles of success, and the students who keep in contact as they move through the grade levels, all reassure me I have made a powerful, lasting impact in the classroom.

As I build my lessons, I ask myself if the students will be motivated. Motivation cannot be accomplished by teaching straight from the instruction book. It is my duty as an outstanding educator to raise the bar. Developing relevant lessons is a pivotal aspect of engaging the students. Whether it is bringing in popular music with lyrics changed to fit content, or giving students real-life problems to help them understand the value of a math skill, relevancy matters.

Early in the school year, I give my students an assignment to write down what they aspire to be when they grow up. I use this information the entire year. I use it as an inspirational tool when describing how specific skills will help them at certain points in their lives. The student who wants to be a basketball player becomes increasingly interested in graphs when I explain he will be able to chart his shooting percentages over the course of his last three games. The student who wants to be a fashion magazine editor pays special attention when I discuss punctuation and spelling.

Expecting the most out of each of my students is a priority for me. I refuse to let my students make excuses for subpar effort. I want them to have the courage to take risks while knowing that I am there to support them if they happen to fail. I ask open-ended questions. I make them show me evidence of their reasoning, and I hold them accountable for their work. I continuously increase the level of complexity of their content in order to take them to a higher level of knowledge.

An outstanding educator is one who will never give up on a student, understands the power of relationships, and insists that children become the best they can possibly be. I live each day by this motto, and believe I make a positive difference in each one of my students' lives.

Despite the naysayers, public education is essential for the foundation of this country. It has been devalued and attacked, especially by the media and so-called experts. This comes from a lack of awareness as to what really goes on inside the walls of our schools.

Contrary to popular opinion, what the public really needs to know is that schools are successful and make a tremendous difference. I have no doubt that I, and the overwhelming majority of teachers, truly matter.

For example, students enter my classroom and school adorned in uniform with tranquil facades, but underneath they are totally broken and scared to death of what the future holds for them. Teachers like myself, one day at a time, put these students back together and give them hope.

One of my former students was a young African American girl with no bed to sleep in, no decent clothing, no food at home. She came into my classroom defiant. She was unwilling to communicate with me or her peers.

However, as with all my students, I was determined to break down her walls. In the mornings, I solicited colleagues to fix her hair. I took her uniforms home and washed them. I sat with her at lunch, listening, giving her a peek inside my world.

I was able to break through. This was most evident when my building principal Mr. Roland came in to evaluate me. Totally unsolicited and unexpectedly, this little girl just had to tell Mr. Roland, "I love my teacher."

He knew her history, so he was stunned and asked her why she loved her teacher. She said, "She cares about me and helps me and wants to see me do good."

Therefore, I feel it is incumbent upon those of us who are truly dedicated and called to eradicate any practice of cutting corners of excellence and accountability. Yes, unfortunately, some of us have been guilty of looking the other way when colleagues have given less than their best. We must all be leaders, and we must demand everyone in this profession put his and her best foot forward. We cannot sit idly by and allow any child to be left behind. It is every teacher's moral duty to give and demand that we all perform at a level of excellence.

Liz Graham, first-grade teacher, 2015–2016

Outstanding teachers foster child-centered classrooms built on strong relationships with students and their families. The children I serve come from difficult home environments.

Structure and stability are not always a given in their day-to-day lives, so I strive to establish security through love and understanding. This means I have breakfast bars stocked for students who come in late and who are hungry. If they're hungry, they won't learn that day. I allow students to check out books under my name because their cards were lost during yet another move. I have let students take naps after I found out their grumpy dispositions came from factors that were outside of their control and prevented them from sleeping.

At the start of each school year, I lay a foundation for a safe environment by asking my students to write our classroom contract. This establishes expectations and examples for the way we should treat each other. I promote a "classroom family" where we support, encourage, and love one another.

Last year, one of my students turned in an assignment to describe something she liked using three supporting details. It read, "I love my teacher. First, my teacher is pretty. Second, my teacher is my teacher mommy. Third, my teacher is love. These are a few reasons why I love my teacher." It brings me a sense of great personal reward to know I'm creating a family within my classroom. Building trust in a child-centered environment allows my students to blossom academically, socially, and emotionally.

Outstanding teachers recognize that connecting with students' families is just as important as connecting with the students themselves. I strengthen parent-teacher relationships by attending birthday parties, dance recitals, sporting events, and even traveling to visit students who have changed schools. Sharing my phone number with parents and students allows me to stay connected seven days a week. Parents are a child's first teacher, and I want to equip them with strategies and tools to help connect them to their child's academic progress.

Throughout the year, I send home individualized information on each child, including skills and activities that need to be worked on. Before summer break, I send students home with practice workbooks and use incentives to encourage completion by the fall. The number of workbooks returned to me on Meet the Teacher Night is impressive. I love seeing the smiles on my previous year's students as they hand me their completed summer goals. Partnering with parents supports my child-centered focus and strengthens parent involvement in their child's education, which encourages a foundation for lifelong learning.

Establishing a child-centered classroom culture is an attribute of a good teacher. However, great teachers extend the "student's needs come first" mentality throughout their whole grade level. The average classroom has a wide range of skill levels. In order to bridge the academic gap, Tulakes developed differentiated learning across my grade level. I have many years experience leading my team as we plan and prepare lessons for these small groups and centers. This technique allows our team to cohesively unite and view every student as "ours." Dividing students into flex groups by skill level allows for individualized child-centered lessons, resulting in greater success. My skill-based lessons and centers include activities and games to promote hands-on discovery of intriguing information. The heart and soul of my classroom is the child-centered climate based on positive relationships and individualization, which allows my students to overcome challenges and fall in love with knowledge and learning.

I hire people brighter than me, and I get out of their way.
—Lee Iacocca, executive

DISCUSSION QUESTIONS FOR CHAPTER EIGHT

1. Have you ever had to meet non-instructional needs of a student or a class? Describe that experience.
2. What is this difference between a teacher and a coach? What do you want to be?
3. How much value do you place on character over capacity? What are the strengths and weaknesses of your approach?
4. Review the Teacher of the Year speeches. How do you balance expectations and empathy when working with a student?
5. What does instilling a "champion" mindset in children look like in your experience?

9

CHARACTERISTICS OF A CAPTAIN

Leadership is a potent combination of strategy and character.
But if you must be without one, be without the strategy.
—General Norman Schwarzkopf, former Commander-in-Chief
of US Central Command

There have already been countless volumes written on the subject of leadership. There have already been countless studies conducted, both quantitative and qualitative on the topic. There are already countless universities the world over that offer courses taught by the most erudite professors on the topic philosophically, ethically, theoretically, religiously, and more. There have already been countless leaders the world over from every field who have been studied, quoted, and dissected since the beginning of time. Yet even with all that has been said, there is not conclusive agreement whether leadership can be learned or if it is an innate gift. I make no claims of being an expert on leadership, but I would like to share principles that have served me well in leading a school turnaround effort.

Those who lead our public schools are in perhaps one of the most undervalued, yet challenging and vitally important professions to the preservation of our nation's democracy. The poor are at incalculable risk without their dexterous leadership. If children are inadequately served in our public schools as adolescents, they are much more likely to inadequately contribute to the good of our country as adults. Regarding the unique leadership role of being a school principal, experience has taught me there should be some non-negotiables.

First, I think it helps if a school leader believes in a higher power. For me, that power is God. You can disagree with me, if you like, but let me tell you why. The work of a principal is extremely demanding and often seems almost impossible. There are incredible expectations from the local school board and superintendent as well as from city, state, and federal officials. These challenges can rise exponentially in our more-challenged schools. The principal has to try to be all things to all people. He or she has to answer to the hierarchy of a central office administration. She has to respond to the perpetual deluge of concerns of teachers. He has to acknowledge the unpredictable concerns of parents. She has to respond to the eerily deep and wide challenges of students. He has to be ready for the drip, drip, drip of community concerns, often finding himself tip toeing in nose-deep water.

Being a man or woman of faith can keep a school leader from drowning in overwhelming circumstances and maintain perspective amid overwhelming need. I prayerfully approached each and every day, and God answered my prayers. He may have said yes, no, not now, or I'm not telling you. But he always answered them.

I needed that. I often lamented to the Lord, and he was there for me.

A Calling

I believe there are some prerequisites and skills that are common to almost any leader, whether a CEO, head coach, politician, pastor, or principal. As they say, "It can be downright scary and lonely at the top." It's definitely not a place for the faint of heart. I believe the principal does not choose the position, but the position chooses him or her. That calling results in both a fit and ultimately success for the schools and children served. Yes, he should have some aspirations to lead. Yes, she must possess the intellect required to perform the duties of the job. But I believe the best principals and leaders are drawn or summoned to their posts. Without a calling, success is a roll of the dice at best.

We all have been told to set our goals high. I too want everyone to be all they can be. I want our children to strive to reach their maximum potential and have probed and prompted students on what they want to be or do when they grow up. However, when it comes to adults, I am not so sure it is a good idea to push people to seek the top position, especially as it pertains to the principalship.

As an adjunct professor at Southern Nazarene University on opening night of my Sociology of Community and Cultures course, I ask each of my students to stand before the class and give their "Why." I want them to look directly at their classmates and tell them why they are aspiring to lead, to become principals or superintendents. My premise for this interrogation is that if their desire is to increase their pay grade, be the boss, or any other reason besides feeling called or driven to impact, reach, or influence beyond their current position, maybe, just maybe, they need to reconsider.

As I stated earlier in the book, my own career plans were to remain in the classroom and perhaps coach football, baseball, and basketball, all of which I love. However, I felt tugged to impact young people in another way and concluded that I could impact more of them as a principal. Moreover, the pool of men, especially of color and with my heart and passion as an administrator, was, shall we say, not abundant. I believe I was called to lead and serve. Thus, I accepted my calling.

Passion

I believe the principal must be a person of passion. I do not suggest this passion has to be manifested in any particular way, but it should be evident and pronounced in some form nevertheless.

My passion is reflected in my face. Some experts contend that body language is 75 percent of our communication. Thus, I smile. I grimace. I look intently. A picture of my face usually says a thousand words as I purposefully try to leave no doubt of my seriousness about my work.

My passion is reflected in my voice. I can hardly contain my volume when I am trying to convey a message of importance and urgency. I often ask audiences when I speak, "What kind of parent would whisper 'no' when witnessing their child about to touch something hot or walk into a busy street. We'd yell, run, or turn flips! We'd do almost anything to warn him or her of impending danger to ensure our message was heard and acted upon." I think it is dangerous and negligent to blandly and impassionately call students, teachers, and parents to give their best. Therefore, I cannot help but raise my voice whether it is an audience of one or one thousand, whether I'm in a closet or on a football field.

To students, I tried to make it clear that respecting their teachers who labored intensively and selflessly for them was not an option. I tried to make it clear that I did not want them to take their learning lightly—that professional sports and entertainment were a one-in-a-million chance and that I personally didn't like those odds. I tried to make it clear that if they did not learn to read (well) that their future outlook was bleak at best. I tried to make it clear that some unbenevolent investors were banking on some of them going to prison. I tried to make it clear that bullying was absolutely unacceptable. I tried to make it clear that if I did it (make decent grades, go to college, and buy a home), they could too.

To parents, I tried to make it clear that the teachers needed and deserved their support, that talking negatively about teachers in front of their children was like handing them a license to be defiant. I tried to make it clear that they needed to make learning a greater priority over sports, having fun, and "chillin." I tried to make it clear that the good old days were gone when children may have been able to slide by without an education because they could get jobs digging holes, pumping gas, sacking groceries, vacuuming homes, and picking up garbage by hand—many of those jobs are now done by machines. I tried to make it clear that their children needed them more than they needed things. I tried to make it clear that their children did not need them to be a friend, but a parent.

To teachers, I tried to make it clear that the good old days were gone where we could say we taught it, but the kids just didn't learn it. I tried to make it clear that student failure was not an option. I tried to make it clear that it was an expectation that every child felt loved and valued. I tried to make it unequivocally clear that I loved and appreciated them for allowing me to be their leader, to push them beyond their comfort zones and be the best collection of teachers in the land.

My passion is felt in my touch. I cannot stand a limp hand-shake or hug—why bother? I extend a firm handshake, a solid high-five or fist bump, or a sturdy, meaningful, heartfelt hug (side-ways if needed). I want my enthusiasm and warmth to convey my message of passion and commitment to students, parents, teach-ers, or anyone else.

Again, I do not have a prescribed method for the demonstra-tion of passion, but I believe that a leader has to bring it to the table, whatever the mechanics. Passion is contagious!

Without passion, how will we motivate our students to learn and continue trying when they find themselves wanting to give up? School is harder than it has ever been. The depth of knowl-edge required of students is much greater today. We do not expect them to just know facts. They must be analytical thinkers, college and career ready. In many cases, the work they take home in fifth grade is difficult, and sometimes their parents cannot assist them. When you couple the academic challenges with less-than-stable communities filled with distractions, students need a principal to give them the oomph needed to keep on keepin' on.

Without passion, how will we challenge people to parent well with all the demands they face today? Parenting is perhaps more difficult now than it has ever been. Parents are stressed trying to provide income in extremely unstable economic condi-tions. Many work more than one job trying to make ends meets. More and more parent alone and have virtually no support network. The advances of technology have too often worked against them, as most children would rather pick up an apparatus to play a game than pick up a book to read. Many of our parents are young and never got some of the parenting, grandparenting, and "village" guidance many of us were blessed to have. They need a principal to give them the oomph needed to best support their children academically, emotionally, and otherwise.

Without passion, how will we inspire teachers to teach and give their best? Teaching is harder today than it has ever been. Teachers are expected to leave no child behind, even when a child, by all indications, seems to say go on without me. Teachers are expected to not be compensated for their true worth, to pay for their own supplies, and to give out of their own pockets for the needs of their students (all of which they willingly do). They are expected to endure in stride the harshest parental complaints and opposition. They are expected to deal with children whose parents can't even control them. They are expected to be above reproach. Teachers are on the front lines, and they need a leader who gives them the oomph needed to perform their jobs day in and day out.

Principals are leaders who must inspire!

I don't think any student, parent, or teacher I have ever known would deny my passion. I was serious about success for all, and I believe every principal must be likewise.

Courage

Principals must display tremendous courage. This attribute is difficult to measure or evaluate. It can often hide behind the mask of logic, reason, and timing. For example, every leader has to decide when to and when not to stand up or stand down. These subjective decisions involve wisdom. However, at the end of the day, every leader knows when he has failed to address an issue because of fear or intimidation.

I'll never forget a shameful occasion early in my career. I was standing with a group of teachers about a half hour after school had ended, just chatting and unwinding. A student came running back into the building, hoping to get back into his class to get his homework he had forgotten. One of the teachers told him it was too late, and he needed to learn to be responsible. I did not agree with it, but I did not protest as I did not want to undermine her in front of others. I failed to be courageous and vowed to never again remain silent when a student was trying to do the right thing. I caved, and I regretted it.

I never ever, ever, ever, ever wanted to be ashamed again because I avoided tough issues. Oh, it was nothing to confront the less tenured, benign, and unpopular staff member that failed to meet an expectation of some kind. It was nothing to stand up to the timid, poor, less-than-influential, voiceless parent who had unwarranted grievances to bear. It was nothing to make a decision that only a few marginal individuals would not embrace.

However, when those faculty members or parents were just the opposite, it can be another matter altogether. But it was my job to show no partiality with regards to concerns or iniquities. Now, confrontation is not something I enjoy or that comes easily for me. I like to push the easy button just as much as the next person. Yet I believed it was my job, if not my moral obligation, to confront issues as needed. Sometimes it meant meeting early in the morning or staying late after school in my office readying for a vitriolic, criticizing, and oppositional parent. Sometimes it meant having a private, difficult conversation with the most well-liked person on the staff. Sometimes it meant making a ruling or change that was without question going to be unpopular. These took courage, and I steeled myself for the difficult tasks and conversations in my calling. It was my job, as in the end I was going to have to look myself in the mirror that night before going to bed. Yes, I owed it to others, but more so, I owed it to myself to do the right thing.

Longsuffering and Forgiving

Every principal or leader should expect some level of disappointment or betrayal, sometimes from the people they might least expect. People say, "It's lonely at the top." They failed to mention that the loneliness can feel like solitary confinement in Siberia. They say, "That's what you get the big bucks for." However, they failed to understand the pay is disproportionately low when you consider a person with so much responsibility, especially compared to police and fire chiefs, bank presidents, and CEOs. Plus, no amount of money seems worth it when you feel like you have been misrepresented, misunderstood, and mistreated by the people you serve.

I am not suggesting a principal should delight in opposition and adversity, nor that responding to such is an easy matter. However, not to expect personal attacks and affliction would be an egregious mistake, or delusional at best, because it comes with the job. Leaders have huge expectations on them, as they should, and they need to have thicker skin than the Average Joe, even if it means faking it until you make it.

My purpose in this book is not to air my personal grievances, but please trust me that I have experienced more than my fair share of workplace antagonism, fraudulence, and enmity from some parents, some staff, and some district-level employees. And to make matters worse, sometimes it hurt even more as it was no doubt connected to the color of my skin. For instance, I was called the n-word by more than a few parents over the years. On two occasions I was physically threatened, and in one of these incidents the individual was holding a claw hammer in hand. My first year at Tulakes, a teacher asked why I even came to the school, as though I didn't belong there. I encountered district support staff who cursed me to my face, and teachers who made slanderous comments and false allegations about me.

But I am not trying to cry "woe is me" here. I am trying to make the point that as the principal and leader, I made a conscious decision to take the proverbial high road in such cases. I apologized to people when I did not wrong them. I greeted people who had no intention of acknowledging me. I prayed for people who in turn spoke ill of me. I never once attempted to use my position or authority to get retribution.

That doesn't mean their treatment didn't hurt or frustrate the dickens out of me; however, as I often say, it is not always right to do what you have a right to do. I had the right and the authority to fight fire with fire, but I wanted my staff to see my character and that I trusted God to fight on my behalf. If I had done the fighting, I might have won some battles, but I doubt I would have won any wars, and I likely would have lost the respect of my staff as well. Also, in my experience, when people see you seek vengeance against one person, right or wrong, they understandably fear you will do the same to them in the right circumstances. A principal must be longsuffering and forgiving.

Servant Leadership

Servant leadership was a buzz phrase a few years ago and one I contend needs to remain abuzz. It is a phrase all leaders need to embrace, but especially so as it pertains to the heart of a principal. As I said previously, at my initial introduction to my staff I informed them that I was there to serve. First and foremost, I tried to demonstrate my servant leadership. I had an open-door policy, and every staff member, from the custodial staff to the most tenured teacher, was welcome to enter and share concerns or needs, great or small. Most took full advantage of my policy. I attempted to assuage any feelings of guilt when they contacted me, no matter how inconvenient it might have been for me. They were encouraged to contact me as needed, day or night, during the week, or on the weekend. I believed I relinquished the right to solitude when I accepted the role of leadership. Another example was when we purchased t-shirts that read, "MBUNTU, I am because we are." I got on my hands and knees with the shirts placed over my back. The assistant principal handed them out one by one as I told the staff they could have the shirt off my back.

I endeavored to practice servant leadership with our parents and students. I caught more than a few parents, especially single mothers, off guard when I would come from behind my desk, remove my tie, and sit on the floor to discuss their sensitive and heartfelt concerns. They were taken aback as they had likely never witnessed any man, especially of professional status, humble himself in such a manner. I did not want to appear that I outranked them in any fashion. Through my actions and words, I made every effort to convince them that I loved their children and had their best interests at heart. They were surprised even more as I volunteered to be held accountable and shared that they and their children were free to share concerns that would be properly addressed.

I also startled many students, especially the new kids to our school who were recalcitrant, ones who had only known glares, stares, and stiff consequences. Sometimes I came from behind that same desk and squatted down to explain that I worked for them. I tried to make it crystal clear that they were my clients, my customers, and my only real purpose at the school. Yes, I was a grown man and the "boss" of the school, but I was there to see that his or her academic and social needs were met. I wish I could have captured their befuddled looks. This type of communication was completely foreign to them. They were so conditioned to only being the recipients of punitive measures. They were speechless.

In general, my staff, parents, and students responded well to being served. In the end, they wanted to know how much I cared, not how much I knew. We forged relationships that made an immeasurable difference in the culture and climate of our school.

Intentional Conversations

To state the obvious, intentional conversations have to be very, well, intentional. A lot of thought has to go into listening and speaking to subordinates and teams of any type. My staff meetings took me much longer to plan and think about than the actual time of the meetings themselves.

I had a desired objective in mind for each meeting. If we were discussing instruction, classroom management, professionalism, or any other best practice, I was always intentional. Prior to our meeting, I might ask certain teachers to be prepared to chime in at a certain point in the discussion or presentation.

On occasion I was known to place chairs and put the entire staff, about fifty people in a big circle. We would just have a "family meeting" and talk about what was or was not happening at our school. If something was broken, it was foolish and unacceptable to just wish or expect it to fix itself. The discussions were candid, sometimes emotional and piercing, but we got "the stuff" out on the table. By the time we left, everybody knew the plan for our ship moving forward and was ready to proceed with great vigor. It was all intentional.

However, the most significant conversations took place one-on-one. I thought of those conversations as mini staff meetings or professional development. I tried to make certain we were all on the same page, same paragraph, and same line. For example, one of my best teachers was also one of the most influential. Sometimes this teacher did not agree with a district or building expectation. On a few occasions, I asked this teacher to use his influence for the good of the entire school, even when he did not agree with the particular decision. But I also listened intently when he had thoughts, and I sometimes heeded his suggestions. I wanted to use my power and influence for the betterment of the school. It was all intentional.

Perhaps one of the best illustrations of my intentional conversations were my annual exit interviews (see in Resources). I held these with each teacher at the end of every year. A portion of the form could be handed in unsigned to maintain anonymity if anyone wanted to communicate this way. Then I also met with each teacher in person to get feedback on me as a leader and to share my thoughts on their body of work for the year.

The overwhelming majority of their feedback for both me and the school were positive and uplifting. They would share that they felt supported by me, which was music to my ears. They gave me thoughts on improving things for the next year, which I was always eager to receive. However, sometimes I did receive negative feedback. I heard complaints someone felt slighted or mistreated. I heard communication could be improved. I heard meetings were too frequent. Sometimes, I was simply able to share a few facts that helped clear the air. Once or twice, we ended up agreeing to disagree. Sometimes, I just had to grin and bear it. I was intentional about making changes on my end.

The overwhelming majority of my feedback for my teachers was also positive and uplifting. I shared my thoughts and appreciation for all their hard work throughout the year, both inside and outside the classroom. But I shared constructive criticism, too. For example, I shared with one teacher that she could be more of a team player. I shared with another that she had more to give and should be more outspoken. I shared with a teacher who needed to employ more best practices. And there were times when I suggested that a teacher should consider other employment options for the following year. It was all intentional.

Hardworking

In addition to being called, anyone who wants to lead must embrace the idea of hard work; there is simply no way around it. Up to this point, I have tried to be very explicit regarding the arduousness of leadership and especially the work of the principal. Again, it is not for the faint of heart. It is often a position of loneliness even in the midst of a multitude. It is not a position of corner-cutting. There are simply never enough hours in the day.

Think of the hard work put in by the head coach of a football or basketball team, especially at the elite level and where winning is expected. There are hours and hours of film to watch, hours and hours of practices to run. There are hours and hours of coaching and counseling. There are hours and hours spent planning and strategizing. Much of their time is spent outside the actual games themselves and is never seen or logged.

As a principal, I rolled up my sleeves and put in the effort, because like any coach, I did not want my team to lose. There was far too much at stake. My teachers, students, parents, and community wanted, expected, and deserved to win. I abhorred the idea of our children's success being predicated on their zip code, family income, ethnicity, race, or other factors beyond their control. Therefore, with few exceptions, I was almost always the first to arrive every morning and the last to leave in the evenings.

On parent conference nights, I tried to make sure that I stayed until the last teacher left. If we had students performing or participating in any event, evenings or weekends, I was almost always in attendance. I wanted my staff and students to know 100 percent that I supported them. If we had an evening event at school that left things extra messy afterwards, I stayed to assist the custodial staff to minimize the extra work and ensure the staff and students could return to a clean building the next day.

During the day, I tried to be in classrooms, in the cafeteria, or accessible to whoever needed me. My reports and paperwork were secondary to the needs of others, which meant that those tasks often got done at home or during non-instructional hours. I more or less worked out a deal with my boss's secretary to call me on my cell phone until I answered, as opposed to leaving a message or emailing when I was needed, because emails were last on my list of priorities, but I always answered my phone.

Ball players do not mind playing hard for a coach who works hard. The same is true of teachers. They do not mind working hard for a principal who works hard.

Love

Without question, a principal or leader needs to have a massive skill set and huge heart to be effective. Many of these attributes have inarguably always been necessities for leaders, but never more so than today. People have so many options today. Their career choices are infinite. They can work in the profit or nonprofit world. They can work from home. They can work for themselves.

With this in mind, when I first became a principal in the early 1990s, teacher candidates were so plenteous that some were leaving the state to get teaching jobs. Universities were supplying a continuous pipeline of competent candidates. Principals had such mountainous stacks of applications that they were known to dispose of some without looking. School leaders definitely had the advantage.

However, today in Oklahoma, teachers can almost pick their district, school, and sometimes even grade. In fact, certified teachers are leaving our state for higher paying jobs at alarming rates. Out of desperation, some schools are now staffed with more uncertified than certified teachers and are having difficulty retaining them. It is now without question a teacher's market.

Yes, the old days are gone, and more is required of a leader or principal today. However, when you consider all that's required, I think the most important attribute of a principal today is something any of us could have—love. If we love the people we serve, the vast majority of them will reciprocate that love.

As a principal, I told my students I loved them, and I tried to demonstrate it everyday. Sometimes it meant telling them loud and proud that I loved them too much to let them fail, to let them give up on themselves, or to let them behave any way less than excellent. It meant showing up for orchestra concerts on evenings and weekends when the sounds they were making could only loosely be defined as music. Love looked like allowing a child to interrupt me in my busiest moment to show me something that made her proud. I put it in my schedule to play basketball the last twenty minutes of the day on Fridays with some of my most challenging students, usually boys. My wife and I gave up our upstairs bedroom to children who needed a temporary place to stay. My wife stood on her feet for hours on end doing girls' hair. My wife and daughter took girls out to shop or get their nails done. My son helped me get OKC Thunder basketball tickets so I could occasionally take students to see Kevin Durant and Russell Westbrook. I visited students in the hospital. I delivered gifts to children on Christmas Day or their birthdays when I knew they were unlikely to receive such from anyone else. Once,

I unwisely went into the middle of a gang fight of more than twenty teens to plead with them to stop fighting because I didn't want them or my students to get hurt. Once, it meant eulogizing three of my students who perished in an apartment fire. This was nothing special, just something you do for the kids you love.

Sometimes, with parents, it meant being the parent they never had and offering counsel when needed. I took parents to get gas and paid for it once we got there. I mediated between estranged parents. I stayed after school for hours with a child when a parent could not be reached and tried my hardest not to be angry when they finally showed up. I went to great lengths to help parents avoid getting their children taken away by the Department of Human Services for circumstantial reasons. I helped parents find food, clothing, and housing. This was nothing special, just something you do for the parents and children you love.

Finally, I told my staff that I loved them and tried to demonstrate it every day. It meant telling them loud and proud that I loved them. I intervened in hostile meetings with parents, enduring the wrath myself. I gathered every resource available to help them in their classrooms. I visited and listened. I texted each one of them a greeting on a holiday when we were out of school. I called and sang "Happy Birthday" on their birthdays. I prayed with them in times of crisis or blessing. I tried to be one of the first people to visit in the hospital when they had a child. Their hurts were my hurts, and their joys were my joys. This was nothing special, just something you do for teachers you love.

Love does. Love acts. I loved those kids, families, and staff, so I tried to do things everyday to show it.

Finally, principals or leaders don't only need to love the people they serve; they need to love their jobs. If they do not have fervor for the work, they won't reach the final goal. And since failure to reach the desired goal in school business means failing the children, this to me is not an option.

I loved my job because I loved my students, parents, and staff. I was known for saying that if I could afford it, I would do my work without compensation. In my twelve years at Tulakes, I never stayed home one day. Over the course of my total career, I did not miss more than three or four days total. I even went to work when district staff were furloughed due to a drastic budget reduction one year. This was nothing special, just something you do for a job that you love.

If your actions inspire others to dream more, learn more, do more, and become more, you are a leader.
—President John Quincy Adams

DISCUSSION QUESTIONS FOR CHAPTER NINE

1. What examples/models of passion have you seen from leaders in your life? How did the passion impact the organization they led?
2. What does passion look like for you? How do you intentionally demonstrate passion?
3. Do you agree with this statement: The principal must be a person of passion. Why or why not?
4. How would you have handled the situation with the student returning for his homework?
5. What do you do when you get feedback that is not favorable?
6. Do you believe teachers, principals, and leaders in general are "called"? Why or why not?
7. Which of the qualities mentioned do you feel you excel at and which do you feel you could most improve?
8. Have you lost your love for the people you serve and

your job? If so, what can you do to re-cultivate this love?

10

NEXT STEPS IN THE JOURNEY

I believe the children are our future
Teach them well and let them lead the way
Show them all the beauty they possess inside
Give them a sense of pride to make it easier
Let the children's laughter remind us how we used to be
—Whitney Houston, "The Greatest Love"

I began this book by sharing about my childhood in order to paint a picture of what it was like for me, and many like me, to grow up poor and Black in Oklahoma. At an early age, I made peace with the fact that I would get my needs supplied but not much more with regard to food, space, or clothing. I also made peace with the fact that learning and experiencing some things that many kids take for granted, like learning to swim, were beyond my reach. We simply had no pools in our community.

I illustrated what it was like for me and many like me to navigate the public education system in Oklahoma. At an early age, I made peace with the fact that the darkness of my skin and the lack of our family's income would prevent me from being the teacher's pet or from being the most popular kid in school. I learned I would not be able to go on field trips, purchase markers and other supplies for science fair projects, obtain band instruments, have transportation to and from baseball or football practice, or have regular school photographs, as my parents were unable to pay for these items.

However, I grew up in a time and with circumstances that afforded me at least a fighting chance of cracking the glass ceiling of my humble surroundings. For one thing, almost everyone around us was in the same boat. None of us had name-brand clothing; everyone wore the same modest clothes. Everyone around us was just trying to make it. They were all a mere paycheck away from being in less-than-desirable circumstances. More important, we all had a sense of family pride and wished and wanted better for one another. I don't think that is the case today.

Moreover, with all of the ugliness of segregation and poverty, there was a positive. Educators, both teachers and principals alike, were highly regarded in the black community. Our schools were filled with black teachers and administrators. They lived in the same communities we did. We attended the same churches and shopped at the same grocery stores. They got their hair cut and curled in the same barber shops and salons. They were biologically related to some of us. Their children attended the same schools. They absolutely cared about us. Our struggles were their struggles.

Therefore, when we failed, they failed. So they pushed and prodded us. They knew our parents by first name, so when we got in trouble in school, we *really* got it at home. The teachers and parents conspired against and for us at the same time. And overall, their work paid off.

In the midst of all the transgressions surrounding segregation, education was a river of hope. That is largely not the case today. Some things are better. Others are worse, much worse.

Finally, in my youth, the number of two-parent households was substantially greater, and there were significantly fewer latchkey children. Therefore, being of color and low income was entirely different. Proportionately, single parents, especially mothers, were not trying to do everything by themselves. Although single-parent homes may be an issue for other ethnic groups, they are disproportionately high for Blacks, and the problem is only getting worse. According to many sources, upwards of 70 percent of our black children do not have their father in the home. The documentary 72 *Percent* shows the dire problem of fatherlessness.

One article about the film puts it this way:

The saddest thing about out-of-wedlock pregnancy in the United States is the children are, for all intents and purposes, fatherless.

A man is more emotionally and financially invested in his children when he lives with them and is married to their mother. Children who don't live with their biological fathers are at higher risk for such social pathologies as out-of-wedlock pregnancies, school truancy and dropouts, and criminality. The majority of juvenile delinquents and adult prisoners grew up in female-headed households. Fatherless children are much more likely to suffer physical abuse, including sexual, because of the men their mothers bring home.[14]

My point in illuminating this dark and dolorous dilemma is

not to project gloom and doom, or to suggest that children raised in single-parent households are all on a collision course with catastrophe. I'm only pointing out that in the past more children were raised in two-parent or extended-family households. That healthy dynamic provided more support for the children who need it most. That is not the case today. These endangered children need our help more than ever.

I retired as the principal of Tulakes in 2016, but I'm still called to help kids. I retired in the hopes that I could help even more kids by encouraging school principals and administrators to be servant leaders for the sake of our kids. In my next voyage, I hope to rally as many advocates as possible to change the narrative for our children. We absolutely need all hands on deck.

I hope to motivate, inspire, and empower teachers, particularly those serving children in our inner cities. Teaching is arduous and often thankless. We have teacher shortages because people don't want to do it. Teachers need a different level of training and to feel valued and supported. They are invaluable to the preservation of democracy and the values of what our country holds dear.

I desire to motivate, inspire, and empower administrators, particularly those serving our families of diversity and poverty. Effectively leading these schools is no small task. The good old days of sitting in an office and "making the big bucks" are a thing of the distant past. Therefore, I want others to know what I know. They don't have to reinvent the wheel. Just take what I have learned and make it better.

I want to motivate, inspire, and empower parents and guardians, especially those who need it most. In many cases, they are paralyzed with trepidation and a lack of knowing how to most effectively advocate for their children, not to mention lacking the tools to nourish them academically and emotionally. I hope to assist them in propelling their children to overcome the odds and low expectations of today's society. I wholeheartedly believe that parents today have their hands full like no time in the history of our country.

I purpose to motivate, inspire, and empower students, especially those at greatest risk, to aim high and go even higher. They don't know what they don't know and are far too often going from day to day with their eyes wide open but failing to see the forest for the trees. I want to champion, push, and spark them into believing in themselves, fighting through the overwhelming traps, snares, peer pressure, and systemic minutia of their finite worlds, and reaching their infinite potential. We are asking students to perform better when things beyond the classroom are growing more challenging every day.

I long to motivate, inspire, and empower universities, churches, politicians, and leaders of all kinds to care and act on the behalf of those who cannot fight for themselves in our schools. They need the expertise, prayers, legislation, and influence of these entities to level the playing field and give these kids a fighting chance.

So what can those who care do next? I humbly submit the following.

Next Steps

Educators can:

- Discuss and implement principles from this book.
- Invite the author to present to staff or consult on training staff.
- Learn, embrace, and implement where applicable Culturally Responsive Teaching.

- Discuss and implement principles from the books *A Framework for Understanding Poverty* by Ruby Payne; *Black Students, Middle Class Teachers* and *100+ Educational Strategies to Teach Children of Color* by Jawanza Kunjufu; and *Teaching with Poverty in Mind* by Eric Jensen.
- Visit schools and collaborate with those who are enjoying a respectable level of success. Don't reinvent the wheel when someone else has already done it.
- Love the people you serve, and love what you do.

Parents can:

- Set high expectations for your child. Make education (learning, appropriate conduct, excellent attendance) of great priority. Be realistic about sports. Not very many of us are raising a Lebron James or Serena Williams.
- Be a role model and hero. Let your child see you overcoming the odds. Keep learning even if it means taking baby steps (one class or course at a time).
- Partner with your child's school. Visit and ask questions, lots of questions. Know your child's teachers. If you are uncomfortable, get someone to accompany you.
- Set high expectations for your child's school. Support the school, but make them aware of you and your child's needs. Ask for help from other parents or past trusted teachers if needed.
- Put your child first and provide as much stability in your home as possible.
- Take advantage of educational technology. Many

libraries and schools offer free access to online
technology.
- Seek assistance from agencies, churches, friends, and
family as needed to support physical and emotional
needs.

Communities and churches can:

- Read, discuss, and embrace principles from *Waking
Up White* by Debby Irving; *Bridges Out of Poverty* by
Ruby Payne, Philip DeVol, and Terie Smith;
Disunity in Christ by Christina Cleveland; and
Under Our Skin by Benjamin Watson.
- Acquaint yourself with schools with populations
described in this book and see how you can
personally help as well as enlist the support of others.
- Find nonprofits or ministries that serve under-
resourced schools and support them with your time
and finances.
- Consider where you reside. If you are willing to send
financial and people resources to help or do mission
work in remote, poverty-stricken territories of South
America and Africa, consider doing the same in
urban areas in North America.
- Vote for representatives who are of the people, by the
people, and for the people.
- Lobby on behalf of schools—financially and
otherwise. We must appropriate more funding,
resources, and support for schools, especially those in
greatest need. Failure to take action on this is going to
lead to an increasingly wide gap between the haves
and have-nots, which is not good for either side.

In closing, I reflect on the collaborative effort and song of USA for Africa in the fight against AIDS, "We Are the World," where some of the most famous names in music (Michael Jackson, Bruce Springsteen, Stevie Wonder, Huey Lewis, Smokey Robinson, Willie Nelson, Tina Turner, Cyndi Lauper, and others), of every genre, race, creed, and color, put egos aside and came together to fight an insidious disease. We also have seen where celebrities have merged their talents and resources for other worthy causes.

We need to come together in the same way for America's children. If it is to be, it is up to you and me. I'm willing to get into a knock-down, drag-out fight for our children. Are you? We need all hands on deck for this gargantuan task, but one of monumental importance for their—and our—future.

Nothing great in the world has ever
been accomplished without passion.
—Georg Wilhelm Friedrich Hegel, philosopher

DISCUSSION QUESTIONS FOR CHAPTER TEN

1. What part of the author's background and experiences resonated most with you and why?
2. The statistics on the realities of the black family and projected outcomes seem dismal and bleak. How do you feel about these alarming facts?
3. The author gives a call to motivate, inspire, and empower various groups of people. How do you see yourself responding to this appeal?

EPILOGUE

I AM CONFUSED!

I delivered the following speech at the University of Oklahoma during the inaugural "This I Believe: OU" event in February 2017.

I am burdened for others, specifically marginalized people of color, primarily because I grew up that way. I grew up amid poverty and little resources. But worse than that, I had little hope. I suffered deprivation without knowing it, only to eventually discover that I was losing in the race of opportunity before I ever got started. Unfortunately, marginalization is as strong today as it ever was. I am confused.

A preacher's kid, I grew up the youngest of six boys, with one sister two years my junior. I went to a school with other children who were all Black and poor just like me, while the more prosperous white children across the street were educated in a better facility that was exclusively for Caucasians. Yes, their homes, cars, churches, and jobs were all superior to ours. Like the television shows I watched—*Leave it to Beaver, My Three Sons, and The Brady Bunch*—life was just better for them. I was confused!

During those same years, I witnessed some of the most tragic events in American history from the eyes of a small child. The first occurred when I was just four years old. I came home from kindergarten to find my mother and aunt watching television, viewing the breathtaking aftermath of the assassination of the President of the United States, John Fitzgerald Kennedy. My aunt and mother were hurting, but the television depicted a dichotomy. Some people in the South, some that didn't look like me, were celebrating. I was confused!

The second event occurred some four years later. Again, I came home from school to see my mom crying. This time a black man was the victim of the unfathomable hate. Dr. Martin Luther King Jr. had just been assassinated. I did not know who he was at the time, but I could tell that he must have been somebody important. The television images and footage are still etched in my mind. I watched the contradicting reactions from people all over the country. Black people were crying and rioting. On the other hand, there were some people of a different hue waving these odd flags I had seen in Civil War movies. Many of them were celebrating. In the days that followed and the tremendous upheaval around the country, the picture became a little clearer. Any and everyone that looked like me was horrified, helpless, and hopeless. But white people seemed to have responses ranging from concerned to exuberant. I was confused!

As time went by, and I became more news aware, I discovered why these men were killed. They spoke up for and dreamed about justice for all. They said that every American had the right to "life, liberty, and the pursuit of happiness." That just made sense to me, and I sure couldn't comprehend why any fellow countryman would kill another for advocating good and justice. I was confused!

Fast-forward forty-plus years, and my fate has been a career in public education, the vast majority as a principal. As I have served in our schools, I have seen many children grow up just like me, not because it was the law, but rather because of systemic issues in our schools and society. Many children of poverty or color are still segregated, with much less chance of achieving the American Dream than others.

You might ask, "How is this so in 2017?" Oh, I am more than happy to explain.

Today, in too many communities, black children are living below the poverty line. Today, in too many cases, children of color are still being suspended from our schools at a dispropor-tionate rate than their non-black peers. Today, children of color, with the greatest needs, are still in schools with the fewest resources. Today children of color have very few people who look like them in positions of authority and influence. Today children of color are in a pipeline to prison. Today children of color are failing and being failed. I am confused.

Fourteen years ago, I inherited a school with a predominately Black and poor student population. It could have been character-ized as a sinking ship with consistently low test scores, lots of suspensions, retentions (students being held back), and other negative indicators. The school is now sailing the uncharted waters of hope and opportunity for all children with some of the best test scores and absolutely the fewest suspensions you'll find anywhere. Why? Because we cared. I am confused.

Finally, today, why are so many of our schools still segre-gated? Today, why are the least still getting the least in our schools? Today, why are so many other schools consistently failing our children of color? Today, why don't enough other people care enough to change things for our children of color? Today, why are there so few schools like Tulakes that are providing places of hope and paths to success for students? Today, why do I have to ask why? I am confused!

What about you?

I carry with me a picture of a child who is near and dear to my heart, my grandson Elliot Jamison Brown. It is my earnest and sincere prayer that he and every other child born in America, "red or yellow, black or white, they are all precious in his sight," has more than a fighting chance at the American Dream. It is thus my sincere prayer that you too have that same prayer and will ultimately put some feet behind your prayer.

ENDNOTES

1. Ed Finkel, "Black Children Still Left Behind," *District Administration*, November 1, 2010, https://www.districtadministration.com/article/black-children-still-left-behind.

2. "Olympic Protesters Stripped of Their Medals," *History.com*, http://www.history.com/this-day-in-history/olympic-protestors-stripped-of-their-medals.

3. Megan Rolland, "Integration Drastically Reduced Oklahoma City Schools' Population," *The Oklahoman*, April 17, 2011, http://newsok.com/article/3558966.

4. Roland Barth, "Improving Professional Practice," *Educational Leadership,* 63, no. 6 (2006): 8–13.

5. Phillip Jackson, "America Has Lost A Generation of Black Boys," March 21, 2006, *The Black Star Project*,

6. Ulrich Boser, "Teacher Diversity Revisited," May 4, 2014, *Center for American Progress*, https://www.american-progress.org/issues/race/reports/2014/05/04/88962/teacher-diversity-revisited.

7. Ruby Payne, *A Framework for Understanding Poverty* (Highlands, TX: aha! Process, Inc., 1996), 41.

8. Sal Albanese, "Education's Elephant in the Room: Poverty," *HuffPost* (blog), July 10, 2013, www.huffingtonpost.com/sal-f-albanese/educations-elephant-in-th_b_3246358.html.

9. Renee Moore in "Response: Teachers Should Dress as Students' Advocate, Not Peer," *Education Week Teacher*, September 14, 2014, https://stockton.edu/education/current-students/documents/faq/FIELDWORK-DRESS-CODE.pdf.

10. Haim G. Ginott, *Teacher and Child: A Book for Parents and Teachers* (New York: Macmillan, 1975).

11. 1 Corinthians 13:11, *The Holy Bible, English Standard Version* (Wheaton, IL: Crossway Books, 2001).

12. Snoop Dogg and Wiz Khalifa, "Young, Wild & Free," *Mac and Devin Go to High School Soundtrack*, The Smeezingtons, 2011.

13. Christopher Bergland, "Tackling the 'Vocabulary Gap' Between Rich and Poor Children," February 16, 2014, *Psychology Today*, https://www.psychologytoday.com/blog/the-athletes-way/201402/tackling-the-vocabulary-gap-between-rich-and-poor-children.

14. "'72 Percent' Documentary on Fatherless Black Children," *Black Community News*, August 6, 2014, https://blackcommunitynews.com/72-percent-documentary-on-fatherless-black-children.

RESOURCES

I've included the bare bones of a few of my MANY forms and communications. These have been stripped down in order to be best communicated in this book. If you would like access to the originals, please go to www.leeroland.education.

I'd love to hear how you adapt these for your purposes!

TULAKES ELEMENTARY EXIT INTERVIEW

Teacher:

Date:

Dear Staff Member,

Thank you very much for your contribution in helping Tulakes to complete a successful 2008/2009 school campaign. Please know that you made a difference and that your efforts are appreciated. To help the administrators prepare for next year, we ask that you carefully consider, answer, and be prepared to discuss the following:

1. Were you successful in reaching your goals for this school year? If not why?
2. How can administration be of greater assistance/support to you next year?

3. Are there any adjustments that you can personally identify to both enhance your success as well as that of the school?

4. What training do you think is needed for staff for 2008-2009?

5. What other ideas, thoughts or suggestions do you have?

TULAKES FATHER'S PLEDGE

What will you pledge for your student?

Name:

Cell #:

Student's name:

Check all that you will commit to:

- I will walk/take my student to school at least once per week.
- I will have lunch with my student at least once per month.
- I will come sit in my student's classroom at least once every 9 weeks.
- I will attend recess with my student at least once every 9 weeks.

- I will read at least one book with my student 5 times per week.
- I will help my student with homework 5 times per week.
- I will talk to my student about what he or she did at school 5 times per week.
- I will attend at least one of my student's extra-curricular activities every 9 weeks.
- I will go on at least one field trip with my student this year.
- I will take my student to the library at least once every 9 weeks.
- I will take my student to get new school supplies or uniforms at least twice this year.
- I will volunteer at my child's school three times this school year.
- I will meet with my child's teachers at least two times this year and support them in educating my child.

Fathers, we want to thank you for your attendance today!
If you would, will you indicate which activity you would be more likely to attend:

Fatherhood Training

Daddy-Daughter Dance

Father-Son Movie/Ball game

TULAKES STUDENT EFFORT GRADE

What is Effort?

Definition of effort:

- A notable achievement
- Use of physical or mental energy
- Hard work
- Intense and careful activity intended to do or accomplish something

How to Put Forth Your Best Effort

- Do your best to arrive at school on time.
- Be prepared with all needed materials.
- Wear your uniform.
- Turn in assignments on time with evidence that you tried your absolute hardest.

- Pay attention. Listen and follow directions the first time they are given.
- Be a great example.
- Be a leader.

Effort Grade Scale

3. In uniform and followed our Tulakes expectations. Had a GREAT day!

2. Needed reminders of our Tulakes expectations and/or partial or no uniform.

1. Received consequences for not following our Tulakes expectations and/or partial or no uniform.

0. Office Referral/In-school Suspension and Parent Contact.

Effort Grade Reward Levels

Gold Level
Daily 3s and a couple of 2s!
Fewer than five 2s

Silver Level
Majority 3s and a limited amount of 2s!
Fewer than 10 2s

Bronze Level
3s and a few 2s
Fewer than fifteen 2s

Effort Grade Parties

Drinks
Popcorn
Pizza
Snacks
Hot Fudge Sundaes
Hot Dogs
Fruit RollUps
Games
Face Painting
Inflatables
Movies
Extra Recess
Dance Parties
Prizes

We BELIEVE you can make all 3s!!

WHAT DOES OUR PASSION LOOK LIKE?

*The kind of commitment I find among the best performers
across virtually every field is a single-minded passion
for what they do, unwavering desire for excellence
in the way they think and the way they work.
Genuine confidence is what launches you out of
bed in the morning and through your day
with a spring in your step.*
—Jim Collins, author

Grade:

Date:

1. When we instruct and interact with **students** our Passion
looks like...

-

-

-

-

2. When we communicate and interact with **_parents_** our Passion looks like...

-

-

-

-

3. When we interact and collaborate with **_colleagues_** our Passion looks like...

-

-

-

-

TULAKES "PEER UP" OBSERVATION AND FEEDBACK FORM

Enthusiasm is one of the most powerful engines of success. When you do a thing, do it with all your might. Put your whole soul into it. Stamp it with your own personality. Be active, be energetic and faithful, and you will accomplish your object. Nothing great was ever achieved without enthusiasm.
—Ralph Waldo Emerson

Teachers,

In an effort to enhance our professional learning community (PLC) at Tulakes, Peer Up is designed to allow you to visit and observe instruction in another *Twister* member's class using this form as a tool. Use this time to observe instruction, either math or reading, giving your partner at least one week's notice. Please remember that this is not for the purpose of evaluation nor is the information to be shared with administrators, but only to enhance best practices, both horizontally and vertically.

STEPS

- Prearrange a 10–30 minute period with your partner, as well as make the necessary arrangements with your team.
- Arrange a time to share your observations within three days of completing the visit.
- Prepare thoughts on the value of this experience to share in a staff meeting.

Check List

- Data-driven instruction
- Empowering students
- Commitment to professional relationships with students
- Professionalism with colleagues

OBSERVATION STATEMENT

Today while visiting your class, I liked/learned/gleaned:
-
-
-

Some ideas I have that you might consider are:
-
-
-

In closing, thank you for granting me the opportunity to learn from you and for allowing me to share my ideas of how to help our school.

Signed:

Dated:

BEHAVIORAL SAFETY NET CHART

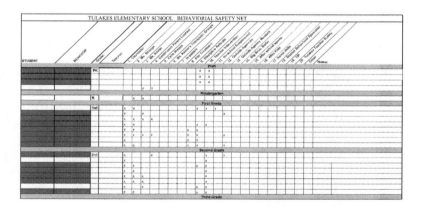

ABOUT THE AUTHOR

Lee Roland has served in public education for more than thirty years, twenty-five of them as an administrator. Particularly gratifying to him are the twelve years he served as the principal of Tulakes Elementary, a high poverty, high diversity, and once failing school (by every significant indicator) that was completely turned around under his leadership.

He now shares his experience with schools, churches, and businesses as a consultant and motivational speaker. Lee also serves as a pastor at the Parish Church in Oklahoma City; a board member for a number of organizations that seek the welfare of children; and an adjunct professor at Southern Nazarene University, where he strives to help future school administrators prepare to truly "leave no child behind."

For more information and to schedule a speaking engagement or training, go to www.leeroland.education.

Made in the USA
Lexington, KY
05 March 2018